Insight Study Guide

Nick Levey

Brave New World

Aldous Huxley

insight

insight

Aldous Huxley's Brave New World by Nick Levey
Insight Study Guide series

Copyright © 2011 Insight Publications Pty Ltd

First published in 2011 by
Insight Publications Pty Ltd
ABN 57 005 102 983
89 Wellington Street
St Kilda VIC 3182
Australia
Tel: +61 3 9523 0044
Fax: +61 3 9523 2044
Email: books@insightpublications.com
Website: www.insightpublications.com

This edition published 2011 in the United States of America by
Insight Publications Pty Ltd, Australia.

ISBN-13: 978-1-921411-82-3

Library of Congress Control Number: 2011931338

Cover Design by The Modern Art Production Group
Cover Illustrations by The Modern Art Production Group,
istockphoto® and House Industries
Internal Design by Sarn Potter

Printed in the United States of America by Lightning Source
10 9 8 7 6 5 4 3 2 1

contents

CHARACTER MAP

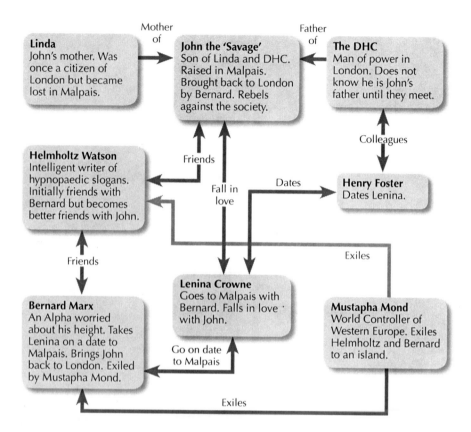

Mother of

Linda
John's mother. Was once a citizen of London but became lost in Malpais.

John the 'Savage'
Son of Linda and DHC. Raised in Malpais. Brought back to London by Bernard. Rebels against the society.

Father of

The DHC
Man of power in London. Does not know he is John's father until they meet.

Colleagues

Helmholtz Watson
Intelligent writer of hypnopaedic slogans. Initially friends with Bernard but becomes better friends with John.

Friends

Fall in love

Dates

Henry Foster
Dates Lenina.

Friends

Lenina Crowne
Goes to Malpais with Bernard. Falls in love with John.

Exiles

Bernard Marx
An Alpha worried about his height. Takes Lenina on a date to Malpais. Brings John back to London. Exiled by Mustapha Mond.

Go on date to Malpais

Mustapha Mond
World Controller of Western Europe. Exiles Helmholtz and Bernard to an island.

Exiles

OVERVIEW

About the author

Aldous Leonard Huxley was born on 6 July 1894 in Surrey, England, to one of Britain's most prestigious scientific families. His grandfather, Thomas Henry Huxley, was a famous biologist and an early champion of Charles Darwin's Theory of Evolution, earning himself the nickname 'Darwin's Bulldog'. Aldous' brother, Julian, was also a famous and successful biologist in his own right, as was his half-brother Andrew. As a teenager, Aldous suffered an illness that rendered him blind for several years, and although he would later recover most of his eyesight, he continued to struggle with this ailment throughout the rest of his life. Perhaps the most immediate effect of this illness, however, was that it steered him away from a career in the sciences that was expected of him and turned him instead towards the life of a writer.

Huxley's interest in a literary career first flourished during his time as a student at Oxford University where he fell in with a famous assortment of radical artists, writers and intellectuals known as the Bloomsbury Group. Other members of this clique included Virginia Woolf, DH Lawrence and the philosopher Bertrand Russell, and they were known for championing what were then radical ideals of free expression and hedonism. It was here amongst the young and fervent intellectuals of England that Huxley set upon his literary aspirations in earnest. After leaving Oxford, he found intermittent employment as a teacher and literary journalist before writing his first novel, *Crome Yellow* (1921), which was a satire of these years spent amongst the young intellectual elite.

In the years that followed, Huxley travelled extensively (and seemingly endlessly) throughout Europe and around the globe, becoming a prolific writer of essays, literary journalism, poetry, travel writing, film scripts and novels. By the time *Brave New World* was published in 1932, his reputation as a unique and important public intellectual who was able to write on nearly any topic he chose was well secured.

In 1937 Huxley settled in the US where he lived until his death in 1963. In these later years of his life he became increasingly interested in esoteric spiritualities and parapsychology. He was also a famous advocate of the use of hallucinogenic drugs. As such, he eventually became an icon of the various 'counter-cultural' revolutions that took hold in America and England during the decades after the Second World War. From beatniks to hippies to punks – all of them read Aldous Huxley, especially *Brave New World*.

While his reputation as a novelist has varied over the years, today Huxley is generally regarded as one of the most brilliant and engaging thinkers of his age. Despite the fact that *Brave New World* was written as an attempt to deal with the social anxieties of the 1930s, its vision of the future still rings true today. Indeed, as Huxley wrote in *Brave New World Revisited*, a collection of essays discussing the themes of the novel, it is frightening how many of the book's predictions seem already to have come true.

Synopsis

In the future year AF 632, the world is a place where human life is genetically engineered and all aspects of society are controlled. Infants are predestined to fit one of five social classes: Alpha, Beta, Gamma, Delta, or Epsilon. At the top of the society, the Alphas are near-perfect human beings, intelligent and physically attractive, yet behave like children in that they avoid anything at all unpleasant in preference for mindless pleasures. At the bottom end of the social spectrum the Epsilons are diminutive and stupid, kept in an infantilised state through birth engineering.

Within this society everyone is conditioned to believe what the World Controllers want them to believe. In place of a god they worship Henry Ford (the initials AF stand for After Ford) and to avoid pain and negative emotions they all take a drug called *soma*. Everyone is constantly happy and has no need to feel pain or sadness. Families no longer exist – people are conditioned to find the idea of 'family' abhorrent, and mandatory birth control stops families from occurring. The society is founded on the belief that social stability is more important than individuality, and a person who thinks for themselves is seen as dangerous.

This seemingly 'perfect' society does have some cracks, however. Physically shorter than the other Alphas, Bernard Marx is an outsider who is self-conscious about his diminutive stature. He is unhappy with doing what is expected of him and raises the suspicion of his superiors with his unorthodox behaviour. We also meet Helmholtz Watson, a writer dissatisfied with the simple party slogans he is forced to produce, and Lenina Crowne, an employee at the Embryo Store who is bored with her present existence.

In an attempt to appear brave and daring, Bernard takes Lenina Crowne on a trip to a 'Savage Reservation' at Malpais, New Mexico. Here amongst the indigenous people they meet John, whose parents were originally citizens of London. Bernard soon realises that John is the secret son of the Director of Hatcheries and Conditioning, a man of great authority in London, and so formulates a plan to bring him back with him in order to shame the DHC out of his job.

Upon his arrival in London, John indeed causes quite a stir. The DHC resigns in shame and people grow equally scared and fascinated by John's 'strange' beliefs. John uses 'smutty' words like mother and father, and believes that people should be free to think and do what they want, including being unhappy. Lenina, despite everything she has learnt about the dangers of deep feelings, falls in love with him.

The longer John spends in London, the unhappier he grows. He violently refuses Lenina's advances and won't let himself enjoy life for fear of endorsing this society he hates. Eventually his mother Linda dies (possibly from an overdose of *soma*) and this sends him over the edge: he seizes a box of the drugs and throws them out a window.

When Helmholtz and Bernard are exiled to an island for their involvement with the riot, John runs away to an isolated lighthouse outside of London. Eventually his location is discovered by tourists who come to gawk at him as though he were a strange beast. Distraught and caught in a confused moral torment, John commits suicide.

Character list

John the 'Savage': the son of Linda and the Director and raised in Malpais, New Mexico; believes in freedom and individuality and is obsessed with the works of William Shakespeare; falls in love with Lenina but won't let himself follow his desires.

Bernard Marx: employee at the Bureau of Psychology, self-conscious about being unusually short for an Alpha; pretends to be brave and different but is really just petty, jealous and cowardly.

Lenina Crowne: attractive and cheerful employee at the Embryo Store; slightly bored with her life; falls in love with John.

Helmholtz Watson: incredibly intelligent and attractive Alpha; writer of 'feelies' and hypnopaedic slogans but wants to produce something more important; initially friends with Bernard but becomes better friends with John.

Mustapha Mond: the Resident World Controller for Western Europe; powerful and confident; was once an individual like Helmholtz but chose leadership over freedom.

The Director / DHC: man of power within London; does not know he has a son until John arrives in London.

Linda: mother of John; was once a citizen of London but became lost on a trip to Malpais; longs to return to the pleasures of civilisation.

Henry Foster: sometime sex-partner of Lenina; intelligent but happy to conform.

Benito Hoover: an always-cheery co-worker of Bernard.

Fanny Crowne: friend of Lenina, they have the same surname but aren't related.

Popé: indigenous inhabitant of Malpais; rapes and abuses Linda; much hated by John.

Darwin Bonaparte: a big-game photographer and filmmaker who works for the Feelie Corporation.

BACKGROUND & CONTEXT

Social change, technology and anxiety

England in the 1930s was a changing and tumultuous place. Still dealing with the effects of World War I, it also had to negotiate the difficulties of the worst economic depression to strike the modern world, which like the Great War was tellingly known as the 'Great' Depression. These two major catastrophes caused many to begin to question the way they had been living. If the world seemed to be falling apart, perhaps they'd been doing something wrong? Perhaps the old world that had seemed so set-in-stone had cracks in it after all? Or perhaps the new changes brought about by the modern world were leading humanity down the wrong path?

The culture in which Huxley wrote his novel was also extremely anxious about the paths that both science and technology were taking. It was a common concern that advances in fields such as genetics and the biological sciences stood to corrupt human nature and lead to things like the genetic manipulation and biological social stratification we see in *Brave New World*. At the time Huxley was writing, people first began to witness the simultaneously magical and terrifying powers technology could invest them with: at the same time as people were able to talk to others across the globe courtesy of the telephone, they were also vulnerable to mass destruction at the hands of machine guns and agents of chemical warfare. Riding high on its achievements, humankind also felt it was teetering on the brink of self-destruction.

Like many others of its time, Huxley's novel seeks to address these anxieties about the course humankind was steering. That *Brave New World* is set in the future is crucial to this purpose. The exaggerated potentials of its world serve as a prophecy of what might come if things are left untended, while providing people with a way to debate the moral and ethical underpinnings of their society.

Utopias and dystopias

Brave New World is considered an example of utopian fiction. A *utopia* is a place 'where all is well', a land or society of peace and harmony, but the term was originally conceived as a pun on such a definition: the word utopia literally means *no-place*, a place that cannot exist. The idea first appeared in literature in 1516 in a work by Thomas More that referred to a fictitious island known as Utopia, governed by peaceful communal policies. While More's is arguably the first example to find its way into literary discourse, it has many philosophical antecedents, perhaps most famously Plato's *Republic*. The 'heavens' of various religions can also be seen as examples of utopias, being places where peace and happiness abound.

To dream of utopia and a better life indeed seems a fundamental aspect of humanity. But while it works well in fiction, in reality it can be much more problematic – hence More's joke about it being an impossible no-place, a world that can never really exist. A *dystopia* (sometimes called a negative or anti-utopia) is the opposite of a utopia, a place where all is *not* well. Dystopian societies are often governed in strict adherence to a particular principle or belief that their rulers think will create the best society, but that in reality oppresses and disenfranchises its citizens. Because of this they are generally defined as having harsh and intransigent governments that subjugate and exploit citizens, allowing them no liberty or freedom. Unlike utopias, we unfortunately have had several real-world examples of dystopias: Stalinist Russia and Nazi Germany to name two.

The interesting thing about dystopias is that they are often simply utopias viewed from the outside or from another perspective. So while a place like London in *Brave New World* might be thought by its inhabitants to be a utopia, to John the Savage it is a dystopia. Often dystopias are simply utopias gone wrong, the other side of the dream of harmony and happiness, and in them we can see the potential dangers in utopian ways of thinking. A true utopia requires its inhabitants to desire exactly the same thing. In this respect it must also be extremely intolerant of difference and individuality, as is the case in *Brave New World*. If a society is good for some, it seems inevitable that it will also be bad for just as many.

Further reading

Other examples of utopian and dystopian fictions include HG Wells' *A Modern Utopia*, BF Skinner's *Walden Two*, Eugene Zamiatan's *We*, Alan Moore's graphic novel *Watchmen*, and perhaps most famously, George Orwell's *1984* (which is discussed in more detail below).

Industrialisation and Henry Ford

The 'Ford' praised in place of God in *Brave New World* refers to the industrialist Henry Ford, the inventor of the first motor car and pioneer of industrial process. The 'T' shape that stands in place of the Christian crucifix refers to the Model T Ford, the first mass-produced automobile and a symbol of the birth of the modern industrial state. The year that the Model T Ford first appeared was chosen 'as the opening date of the new era' (p.52), and so we can work out that the year in which the novel is set, AF 632, is equivalent to AD 2540.

Ford was famous for developing the 'assembly line' style of mass-production and his industrial practices definitely inform the workings of *Brave New World*'s Central London where people are assembled like machines. At one stage the Bokanovsky Process is even celebrated as 'the principle of mass production at last applied to biology' (p.7). Ford's industrial example is thus in many ways the inspiration for the society, the principle upon which it is built.

Huxley seems both fascinated and appalled by the Fordian potentials of modern technology. He describes the 'assembly line' in great detail (especially in Chapters One and Two), which suggests that for him these technologies and industrial processes possess an almost otherworldly, magical power. But the fact that they are responsible for breeding such a rigid and lifeless humanity, and that machines effectively become people's 'parents', also implies his anxiety about the way technology can penetrate and control our lives.

Behavioural Psychology and conditioning

Brave New World engages with many of the popular philosophical and scientific ideas of its time, especially in the field of psychology. The scene in Chapter Two, in which the infants are taught to fear flowers by having the flowers associated with electric shocks, is a clear reference to the work of the Russian physiologist Ivan Pavlov, who conducted a famous series of experiments in order to demonstrate what he referred to as 'Classical Conditioning'. By associating the presence of food with the sound of a bell, Pavlov was able to make a group of dogs react the same way to the sound of the bell as they would to the presence of food. This demonstrated that two entirely unrelated stimuli can become intertwined in the brain. In Huxley's novel there are many examples of this sort of conditioning. Through the intermingling of flowers and pain, the infants from Chapter Two learn to avoid nature just as an individual naturally wants to avoid pain.

Although Huxley's book predates the work of BF Skinner, the type of conditioning experienced by the infants is also similar to the kind Skinner demonstrated with his device known as a Skinner Box. Interestingly, Skinner also wrote a classic utopian novel called *Walden Two*, which was influenced by Huxley's book.

Psychoanalysis and Sigmund Freud

Another of *Brave New World*'s influences is psychoanalysis and the theories of its founder Sigmund Freud, which were immensely popular in the years that Huxley was writing. At one stage in the novel Freud is referred to as 'Our Freud', the name Henry Ford took 'whenever he spoke of psychological matters' (p.39). Freud famously formulated a view of humanity that saw people as ruled by the tension and anxiety caused by repressed and socially unacceptable desires. Freud believed that the mind was separated into Conscious and Unconscious areas, and that most of our mental life was hidden away in the Unconscious parts of the brain, which we could only access through the analysis of our dreams (for anyone interested in psychoanalysis, Freud's *The Interpretation of Dreams* is a fascinating and important text).

Freud also believed that our lives were structured by an inner conflict, which he named the Oedipus Complex. A reference to *Oedipus Rex*, a play by the Ancient Greek poet Sophocles in which a king named Oedipus discovers that he has unknowingly murdered his father and married his mother, Freud believed that every young boy holds a deep and unconscious attraction toward his mother and feels a violent rivalry toward his father, whom he thinks has stolen his mother's attention away from him. In many ways Freud's theory is a description of how the mind of a child experiences the pain of growing up: as the son ages and his mother naturally needs to look after him less and less, he grows resentful at this newfound lack of attention, and so lashes out at his parents for the hurt he feels has been done to him.

In *Brave New World*, this Oedipal schema is played out in the relationship between John, his mother Linda and her lover Popé. John is infatuated with Linda and filled with violent rage at the thought of Popé, thinking that Linda has abandoned him for her lover. John's later rage at the whole of London can also be seen to represent his anger at his real father, DHC Tomakin, whom he also unconsciously considers to have abandoned him.

Mustapha Mond states that 'Our Freud had been the first to reveal the appalling dangers of family life' (p.39). The society of London, knowing the instability such psychological problems present, has tried to entirely eradicate the family unit as a way to avoid the inner turmoil of the Oedipus Complex altogether. One of the many dangers that John presents to the society, then, is the return of the family unit. His presence reveals that it still persists.

It is possible that Huxley saw Freud as the Henry Ford of psychology – someone who would reduce human complexity to assembly-line parts. His treatment of Freud in *Brave New World* might have been an attempt to anticipate and lampoon the kind of reading that would have been *de rigueur* (necessary protocol) for intellectuals in the 1930s.

George Orwell's *1984*

While Huxley's book was written sixteen years earlier, it is important and useful to consider *Brave New World* alongside George Orwell's classic dystopian novel *1984*, which has many similarities as well as crucial differences. Orwell's dystopian vision of a future ruled by a mysterious organisation/figurehead known only as 'Big Brother' is similar to *Brave New World* in that it envisages a civilisation controlled by an untouchable form of government that conditions its citizens into believing what it wants them to believe. But Orwell's novel depicts a much more nihilistic and depressing world. While *1984*'s Oceania is a bleak and drab dystopia, some aspects of Huxley's vision of the future actually do seem quite good: the reduction of pain and availability of free medical treatment seem to be what every society strives for.

Perhaps the best way to account for the differences between *Brave New World* and *1984* is to consider that Huxley's text is almost exclusively told from within the highest echelons of the society (the elite Alphas), while Orwell's protagonist, Winston Smith, is a lowly worker with no freedom or right to self-determination. Most simply, *Brave New World* is a view from the top down, while *1984* is a view from the bottom up. Life for characters like Bernard and Lenina does indeed seem quite good at times; they are allowed some degree of freedom and are clever enough to be able to think for themselves. But if the story were told from the perspective of a lowly Epsilon trapped unthinking on a production line, it might indeed seem quite different.

Another important difference is the contrasting way the societies are governed. While it is difficult to view the actions of *1984*'s Big Brother as anything but violently oppressive, in Huxley's vision of the future the ruling class's means of control are decidedly more subtle. As Huxley wrote in a letter to Orwell, rather than the dictatorial 'boot-on-the-face' policy of aggressive social control, the leaders in *Brave New World* use much more effective and subtler processes of coercion to keep citizens in check. Rather than forcing people into following a party policy, they brainwash them into 'loving their servitude' (quoted in Baker 1990, pp.22–23). Huxley believed that it was due to this difference between the two books that his would prove to be the more accurate vision of the future, and the more horrific. A world where one cannot even begin to see that there is an enemy to be fought against is supremely terrifying.

Shakespeare

Brave New World is full of references to the plays and sonnets of William Shakespeare – even its title is taken from a character's speech in *The Tempest*. John frequently quotes Shakespeare and uses his words to help him understand situations and make decisions, in much the same way as the citizens of London recite their hypnopaedic lessons. With John's reliance on Shakespeare, Huxley (somewhat jokingly) makes the reader question the extent to which we have been similarly influenced by the great texts of our culture.

The main plays that John quotes from are *The Tempest*, *Othello*, *Hamlet* and *Romeo and Juliet*. While it's not essential to have read them in order to understand *Brave New World*, they can help you bring new perspectives to the book.

Useful link

Wikipedia contains a helpful collection of all the Shakespeare quotes used in *Brave New World*:

http://en.wikipedia.org/wiki/List_of_quotes_from_Shakespeare_in_Brave_New_World

GENRE, STRUCTURE & LANGUAGE

Genre

The 'novel of ideas'

Huxley's books have often been called 'novels of ideas,' dramatisations of the various philosophies, social theories and anxieties current to their time and place. As such, a great deal of *Brave New World*'s plot and drama occurs in dialogue between characters, rather than in 'action'. Indeed, if one were to summarise the novel's plot based on its action – or what 'happens' – it might only take a few simple sentences, but to represent the breadth and significance of its ideas would easily fill many books – and it has (see the References and Reading section for a few examples).

Science fiction

Because of its imaginative depiction of a future world, especially its focus on new technology, *Brave New World* best fits the genre of science fiction. The term 'science fiction' encompasses a wide range of texts including such works as HG Wells' *War of the Worlds*, Mary Shelley's *Frankenstein*, and George Lucas' *Star Wars* films. Usually it is defined by a preoccupation with imagining the future and the various social, technological and ecological changes that might occur, or imagining the strange realities brought about by humankind's advances in scientific knowledge.

It's easy to see how *Brave New World* fits this genre. It tries to predict what the future might look like, and does this with a focus on the technology and scientific procedures with which the society is able to construct its ideal citizens. As well as these aspects, *Brave New World* also employs other common science fiction elements, namely the story of an 'alien' (in the form of John the Savage) visiting the planet earth (represented by London). While John is obviously not the extraterrestrial this term usually implies, to the citizens of *Brave New World* he may as well be – he is strange and different and the people react to him as if he were not even human. In the novel we get to see both sides of this otherworldly 'visitation': we readers, along with John, witness a strange and futuristic society, and we also see what happens when a stranger from another world enters this place.

Utopia or dystopia?

Huxley's novel more specifically fits into a niche within science fiction known as utopian or dystopian fiction (for a definition of utopia and dystopia see the Background & Context section above). The question of whether *Brave New World* presents a utopia or dystopia speaks to the heart of the novel, and deciding which, if any, category it falls into will be crucial to how it is interpreted. Huxley ensures that this is never an easy decision to make: at some points London seems drab and austere; at others it appears full of life and excitement. The book, in this way, forces the reader to actively engage with the ethical debates at its heart to try and come upon their own solution. It makes us question our own beliefs too: is happiness more important than freedom? Can you be truly happy if you don't have the potential of being sad? If there is no risk of harm, if every negative emotion can be dreamt away on a *soma* holiday, then can anything truly be considered *good*? These kinds of oppositions pervade almost all areas of *Brave New World* and are one of the reasons it is such a rich novel, one that demands that its readers interpret it carefully.

Structure & Language

Contrapuntal form

Huxley developed a writing style he referred to as 'contrapuntal form', and understanding this is important in grasping how *Brave New World* works as a novel. 'Contrapuntal' is a term taken from musical theory that refers to the juxtaposition of different and opposing melodies or rhythms in order to form a complex and interwoven tapestry of competing themes, harmonies and disharmonies. In his earlier novel *Point Counter Point*, Huxley described this technique as follows: '[a] theme is stated, then developed, pushed out of shape, imperceptibly deformed, until, though still recognisably the same, it has become quite different' (Huxley 1963, p.408). *Brave New World* is full of examples of this method. For instance, the character Bernard Marx starts off desiring freedom and despising the culture of London. As the book progresses, however, his objections begin to be revealed more truly as bitter resentments for a society he feels has excluded him because of his diminutive height. What had initially appeared, in the early stages of the book, as a genuine moral objection to the society, is eventually revealed to be a selfish way of getting attention. The way that Bernard's objection to the society is gradually complicated and exposed as something different from its initial appearance is typical of many other 'contrapuntal' themes in *Brave New World*. Other instances include the frequent use of ironic juxtapositions and the complicated treatment of the idea of individuality. Huxley's use of contrapuntal form ensures that every argument has two opposing sides, and that we have to take care when considering characters and themes so as not to misrepresent them.

Imagery and symbolism

When Huxley describes a location or an object it is rarely just a neutral description. He often invests passages that describe the weather and other forces of the natural world, for example, with symbolic or metaphoric value. When Bernard and Lenina fly in his helicopter above the ocean, with the wind and clouds and 'black foam-flecked water heaving beneath them' (p.90), the description of the ocean and the wild weather are representations of the tumult that Bernard feels within himself, and also symbolic of the uncontrollable forces of nature that Bernard (at this stage of the book) thinks he desires and feels more at home in.

In accordance with the contrapuntal elements of Huxley's technique, another of his favourite ways to use language in *Brave New World* is to set up juxtapositions of imagery. This frequently occurs in the early chapters of the book where the strangeness of the society needs to be established quickly and effectively. In one example a description of the native flora and fauna is given:

> The roses were in bloom, two nightingales soliloquized in the boskage, a cuckoo was just going out of tune among the lime trees. The air was drowsy with the murmur of bees and helicopters. (p.30)

The inclusion of helicopters as if they were of the same ilk as birds and bees actively asserts how bizarre this world appears to us. Huxley doesn't just tell us that things are different, he *shows* us. This use of juxtaposition recreates within us readers the same feeling of shock a stranger would experience when entering this world.

Narrative voice and point of view

Brave New World has a very active and fluid narrative point of view that moves frequently between characters, ensuring that we always see different sides to a situation. The narrative voice is omniscient, hovering above all the characters, but it can also closely follow the thoughts and feelings of any given character that is in focus. Towards the end of Chapter Three the narrative point of view begins to switch rapidly between different scenes. Eventually this happens so quickly that every sentence is from another character's perspective and location. The effect is like listening to several conversations all at once and Huxley uses it to create unexpected ironies and comparisons between viewpoints.

CHAPTER-BY-CHAPTER ANALYSIS

Chapter One

Summary: *Introduction to the civilisation of Central London in the future year AF 632. A group of students is taken on a guided tour of the Central London Hatchery and Conditioning Centre.*

From its first sentence *Brave New World* works hard to tell us that this is not the world as we usually know it. It opens with a simple description: 'A squat grey building of only thirty-four storeys', as if thirty-four storeys were unusually small (p.4). Though it is summer, a 'harsh thin light' contributes to the 'wintriness' of the laboratory inside. Its workers are described as sterile and inhuman, dressed in 'corpse-coloured' clothing, giving no impression of 'living substance' (p.4). It's a bleak and lifeless picture. Then the book provides us with an ironic joke to really emphasise the strangeness of the scene: '"And this," said the Director opening the door, "is the Fertilising Room"' (p.4). That such a sterile place is where fertilisation – the making of life – happens, makes us see what a strange world this truly is.

This first chapter is essentially a tour through a 'factory': we accompany the Director of Hatcheries and Conditioning (or DHC for short) and his colleague Henry Foster as they take a group of students on a guided tour of the facilities. This is a useful narrative device, as it provides a natural way of describing the abnormalities of this world to us – we readers are learning just as the students are. This is a place where people are not born but raised through a complex process of genetic engineering that, among other things separates them into strictly defined social classes.

Key point

It is already clear that in this world a person has worth only according to what use they are to society; they are produced and valued much like a tool or a machine.

> **Q** Is there something wrong with treating humans like everyday commodities?

Chapter Two

Summary: *Inside the Decanting Room; infants conditioned to avoid the distraction of books and botany; hypnopaedia is described.*

If the first chapter described the physical control of human life, this next describes the control of the mind. At first the inside of this Decanting Room seems the direct opposite of the wintry Hatchery and Conditioning Centre: full of life and colour, 'very bright and sunny' (p.19). But it is all to the same purpose in the end, for this is merely another 'factory' designed for artificially constructing humans. The natural desire of the children to move towards the pretty and shiny things is the 'problem' that must be trained out of them.

The unflinching manner in which the DHC gives his commands to shock and terrify the babies with alarms and electric currents reveals his tacit view of these lower-caste humans: they are things that need to be controlled, and their howls of terror have no impact on him. Rather, they are examples of this society's brilliance: he speaks 'triumphantly' (p.21) as he directs the students' attention to the children who are now too afraid to approach the things of beauty. The infants are little more than animals or machines to him, their wellbeing subservient to the society's overall goal of stability.

Key point

'What man has joined, nature is powerless to put asunder' (p.29). This is one of the most important quotes in the book and suggests a belief that humankind has grown more powerful than the world of which it is a part. It thinks it has conquered nature, but has perhaps forgotten that it will always be part of it. Huxley has turned a biblical quote on its head: 'What God hath joined together, let not man put asunder' (Matthew 19:6).

Q Is it acceptable, as the DHC believes, to treat the infants badly if it makes them good citizens later in life?

Chapter Three

Summary: *Children engaged in 'erotic play'; material consumption as a means to a greater social good; introduction of Mustapha Mond, Bernard Marx and Lenina Crowne.*

As discussed earlier, in the opening of this chapter Huxley sets up an ironic contrast: 'The roses were in bloom, two nightingales soliloquised in the boskage, a cuckoo was just going out of tune among the lime trees. The air was drowsy with the murmur of bees and helicopters' (p.30). It's another humorous and ironic image intended to emphasise the artificiality of this world. Amidst this poetic description of the flora and fauna are 'helicopters' as if they were as much a part of the natural scenery as birds and bees.

The general purpose of this chapter is like the previous two: to establish the different beliefs of its citizens, and in many ways these first three chapters mimic the maturation process of the human organism. We first started off with the embryos, then met the infants in Chapter Two, and now we are amongst the young adults to see what processes they have been subjected to in order to maintain a stable society.

As Huxley introduces us to both Mustapha Mond and Bernard Marx, he uses the actions of others toward them as a way of economically describing who they are in the social world of London. The DHC '[springs] to his feet' (p.33) at the sight of the Resident Controller for Western Europe; Henry Foster and his friend '[turn] their backs on Bernard Marx' (p.34), a strange and ostracised member of the Psychology Bureau. It's clever writing by Huxley and ensures we instantly form an active impression about these characters, with minimal effort. Mustapha is powerful and his voice sounds like 'a trumpet' (p.42). Bernard is someone to be avoided, a man of 'unsavoury reputation' (p.34). The reason for this, we learn, is that Bernard thinks differently from the norm. As an Alpha he has some power to form his own thoughts, and feels he has outgrown the restrictions of the society, and we begin to sense that Bernard might perhaps become the hero of the novel, the one who will rebel against its mechanisms of control.

Typical again of Huxley's contrapuntal style, which juxtaposes opposites, Mustapha Mond provides us with information that begins to complicate the largely negative picture that has been drawn of this society so far. Mond believes that the society's firm ideology of '[n]o civilisation without social stability' (p.42) is not just to be taken as the manifestation of a will to power, but a practical response to the failures of the past, an attempt to prevent such disasters as famine and the 'Nine Years' War' occurring again (p.47). This is his justification for the extraordinary measures of control practiced by this civilisation. It may be a place without freedom, but, as he sees it, it is 'a choice between World Control and destruction' (p.48).

Q Is social stability worth a lack of individual freedom?

Chapter Four

Summary: *Lenina agrees to go with Bernard to visit the 'Savage Reservation' in New Mexico; Bernard visits his friend, Helmholtz Watson.*

For the first time we are introduced to one of the society's lowest classes, an Epsilon-Minus Semi-Moron operating an elevator. He is 'a small simian creature' (p.58) stuck in a 'dark annihilating stupor' (p.59), not much more than an animal.

This chapter focuses on the personalities of Bernard Marx and his friend Helmholtz Watson. Bernard is riddled with self-consciousness and social anxiety because of his diminutive stature, worrying that his Alpha status is not respected. His 'physique [is] hardly better than the average Gamma' (p.64), and he is shamefully forced to look them in the eye rather than down at them from a height. He's a classic sufferer of 'short man syndrome'. Perhaps, then, his dissatisfaction with the state of Central London is just to do with the fact that he doesn't seem to fit in.

Like Bernard's defects, Helmholtz Watson's excess of ability has similarly made him an outsider. Helmholtz is the direct opposite to Bernard, tall and well built and popular with women. But because of his extreme intelligence he is also left dissatisfied with the world, looking for something more.

Q Does being an outsider to a society mean more than just 'not fitting in'?

Q A few of the main characters are dissatisfied to some extent. Does this suggest the society is not as stable as it seems?

Chapter Five

Summary: Lenina and Henry continue their flight over the city and return to Henry's apartment; Bernard attends an 'orgy' at the Solidarity Centre.

As Lenina and Henry fly over the city they discuss what it must be like to be a member of one of the 'ant-like' lower castes, deciding that it must be acceptable because the people of those castes 'don't know what it's like being anything else' (p.74). Considering what we've seen of the 'simian' Epsilon elevator operator in the previous chapter, who seemed resolutely happy despite his trivial job, it seems a difficult point to argue against, even though it feels incorrect.

When Lenina says 'I'm glad I'm not an Epsilon', Henry replies that even if she were 'your conditioning would have made you no less thankful that you weren't a Beta or an Alpha' (p.74). We are beginning to learn that we cannot necessarily trust or take as natural the opinions the characters express, because they are opinions that have been learnt through hypnopaedic brainwashing. To take another example: '"Yes, everybody's happy now," echoed Lenina. They had heard the words repeated a hundred and fifty times every night for twelve years' (p.75). Can we really trust that everyone truly is happy as Lenina claims, or is this merely what they've been taught to think? Does the fact that some people (such as Bernard and Helmholtz) are dissatisfied with their lives, wanting something more, suggest that maybe deep down they are not happy?

Key point

Soma raises 'a quite impenetrable wall between the actual universe and their minds' (p.77) which seems to suggest that these people live in a constant state of illusion. Can we truly trust anything they feel?

Q Should the Epsilon semi-morons still have the same freedom and rights as an Alpha?

Q Is the only reason Lenina and others seem happy because they've been brainwashed?

Chapter Six

Summary: *Lenina worries over her decision to travel to New Mexico with Bernard; Bernard visits the DHC and is told the story of his fateful trip to the Reservation; Lenina and Bernard travel to New Mexico.*

We're beginning to learn more about Bernard. He wants to go for 'walks in the Lake District' (p.89), which was a favourite activity of the British Romantic poets like William Wordsworth. He wants to be alone and prefers the reality of misery rather than the artificial happiness of *soma*: '"I'd rather be myself," he said. "Myself and nasty. Not somebody else, however jolly"' (p.89).

As he flies his helicopter back home with Lenina, he stops over the ocean, identifying with the uncertainty of the waves, the 'black foam-flecked water heaving beneath them' (p.90). The wild ocean is a symbol for the rebellion he desires, a force uncontrolled by society, moving in whatever way it wants. He says it makes him feel 'as though I were more me' (p.90). This view of the ocean is exhilarating for him, but terrifies and confuses Lenina who is much more a product of her world. She cannot understand what Bernard feels.

The story the DHC tells Bernard about his trip to the Reservation excites him, makes him respond 'almost enviously' (p.97). What's significant about the story is not just that it foreshadows plot information that will be revealed later in the book (that Linda was the woman the Director lost in the Reservation), but that it's a tale about the powerful, uncontrollable forces of nature. The reason the DHC lost his companion was because of a 'most frightful thunderstorm' that 'poured and roared and flashed' (p.96). While he intends the story to be a warning of the dangers of the 'uncivilised' world, this description of being at the mercy of the wild forces of nature only makes Bernard want to visit the Reservation more. The place is a symbol for the freedom Bernard claims he desires, a world where one can still 'feel something strongly' (p.94).

Typical of Huxley's writing style, however, this picture of Bernard as a brave rebel not content with the status quo is almost immediately undercut. When Bernard finds out through Helmholtz that the DHC has threatened to exile him to Iceland, he retreats from his earlier stoical bravery, and faced with the real threat of facing hardship and being deprived of *soma* he realises that 'not a trace was left' of his rebellious bravado (p.104).

Q Is Bernard in love with the idea of being different more than the reality of it?

Chapter Seven

Summary: Bernard and Lenina begin their tour through the Reservation at Malpais; description of an indigenous ritual; introduction of the 'Savage' John and his mother Linda.

The complex portrayal of Bernard continues in the scenes at the Reservation in Malpais, New Mexico. As Lenina grows shocked at the spectacle of 'two young women giving breast to their babies' (p.111), he deliberately acts as if her discomfort is trivial and that he is above it: '"What a wonderfully intimate relationship," he said, deliberately outrageous' (p.112). But we of course know that Bernard is only affecting this bravado because he has grown ashamed 'of the weakness he had displayed that morning in the hotel' when he had worried about being exiled. He is going 'out of his way to show himself strong and unorthodox' (p.111). Pulled and pushed about by social expectations and self-consciousness, Bernard seems to have no inner integrity.

John the 'Savage' appears the opposite of the 'civilised' norm. He actually wants pain and suffering rather than happiness, wants to be hit by the whip in the mysterious ceremony, and thinks good will come of this. In many ways John is a symbol for the failure of mankind to control nature. His conception was an accident, a miracle that subverted the technology put in place to stop it. His mother Linda '[does] not know how it happened' (p.120), for she had followed all the contraceptive procedures. In being the child of the failure of technological control, John is a living testament to the power of nature to subvert man's intentions.

Q Why is Lenina shocked by John's behaviour?

Q Can we continue to trust what Bernard says, or is he always just trying to impress someone?

Chapter Eight

Summary: *John tells Bernard about his childhood; Bernard contrives to bring John back to London.*

John remembers all the hardships from his childhood, how he discovered 'Time and Death and God' (p.136). The rape of his mother angers him, the loss of his love Kiakimé saddens him. He also remembers the utopian descriptions of London that Linda would impart, how she described it as a place free from all the hardships of the Reservation. John tells Bernard how his life changed when given the *Complete Works of William Shakespeare* as a child. He finds a mirror to his own life in the passages from *Hamlet* (pp.131,133), a way to make sense of the world. He is an outsider to the Indian civilisation, never truly allowed into its rituals and customs; but in the words of Shakespeare he finds his own 'religion', a way to feel connected to the world around him. While the Indians have their sacred practices, John now has his own 'magic'. This chapter is full of quotes from Shakespeare. Indeed, they seem to make up most of John's speech throughout the book. The title of the novel comes from lines he quotes from *The Tempest*.

Upon hearing John's stories Bernard feels he has found someone just like himself, someone who knows what it is like to feel 'rather different from most people' (p.137). Yet there is another motive to his plan to bring John back with him to London; it is 'the first move in a campaign whose strategy he [has] been secretly elaborating ever since [...] he realised who the "father" of this young savage must be' (p.138). Bernard wants to blackmail the DHC into not banishing him to Iceland.

Q Does John relate to the works of Shakespeare in the same way a religious man relates to the words of 'God'?

Q How has our understanding of Bernard changed from when we were first introduced to him?

Chapter Nine

Summary: Lenina takes a soma holiday; Bernard gets approval from Mustapha Mond to bring John and Linda back to London; John breaks into Lenina's rest-house.

Bernard grows delighted as his plan starts to come to fruition. 'Thoroughly enjoying himself' (p.142), he is excited not just about exposing the Director's shameful secret, but also about gaining attention. When John breaks into Lenina's room we begin to see that he is ruled by dramatic, theatrical passions, even to the point of being dangerous. He is transfixed by her beauty, but then overcome with shame about what he intends to do to her. He is caught between extremes, like a Shakespearean character himself. The plays he quotes from in this chapter are *Troilus and Cressida* and *Romeo and Juliet*.

Q Can the plays of Shakespeare help us to understand John's behaviour? Does he use Shakespeare's words in the same way that others recite hypnopaedic slogans?

Chapter Ten

Summary: Back in Central London, the Director is getting ready to punish Bernard; Bernard surprises the Director by introducing Linda and John, causing hysterical laughter from the many onlookers.

As he prepares to punish Bernard for his anti-social behaviour, the Director discusses with Henry Foster some ideas crucial to the civilisation of London. He says that 'it is better that one should suffer than that many should be corrupted'. The individual is a threat: 'unorthodoxy threatens ... Society itself' (p.148).

The scene that unfolds when Bernard introduces Linda and John seems to suggest his plan has worked: he has, for the moment at least, escaped punishment through embarrassing the Director. In the Fertilising Room 'test-tubes of spermatozoa were upset' (p.151) and the workers shriek and laugh at John's use of such smutty words as 'father' and 'mother', showing that already his presence has begun to disrupt the strict order of the society.

Key point

At the beginning of the chapter everything was 'in ordered motion' (p.146), the image of four thousand clocks all striking exactly the same time emphasising the uniformity of the scene. By the chapter's end, however, it has descended into chaos, with workers falling over in laughter and tears. John is clearly threatening to disrupt the strict order of this world already.

Q Why does John's presence cause such disorder?

Q Is the DHC's embarrassment cowardly? Should he have stuck up for his newfound son?

Chapter Eleven

Summary: The Director has resigned from his job in shame; Bernard becomes famous and takes John on a tour of London; John grows increasingly worried about Linda's soma holiday; Lenina takes John to the 'feelies'.

When Bernard takes John on a tour of the city, all of 'upper-caste London was wild to see this delicious creature' (p.153). We see the childishness of the Alphas and Betas in the giggling and finger-pointing that John meets everywhere. Ridiculing 'otherness' is an everyday process here, as we can judge by the early treatment of Bernard, of Linda upon her return, and even of the powerful DHC when he is publicly humiliated.

As Bernard begins to garner fame and favour, once again we see what a weak and hypocritical person he is. Despite his earlier contempt for promiscuity, Bernard now brags to Helmholtz Watson that he 'had six girls last week' (p.156). Helmholtz is 'rather sad' that Bernard has turned out not to be truly different (p.157). All Bernard needed to be happy was for other people to like him. Helmholtz, on the other hand, already fits in – he is handsome and tall and popular, but still feels that he doesn't belong. As success '[goes] fizzily to Bernard's head' (p.157), Helmholtz feels like he has lost a friend.

Q Has Bernard's dissatisfaction with the world really just been anger at the fact that he doesn't fit in?

Chapter Twelve

Summary: *Bernard's 'bubble' bursts as John refuses to attend his party; Mustapha Mond censors an essay about biology; Helmholtz and John become good friends and bond over Shakespeare.*

The 'Savage' is having a profound effect on Lenina, turning her into an outsider of sorts, too. If, as Mustapha Mond said in Chapter Three, feeling 'lurks in that interval of time between desire and its consummation' (p.44), then Lenina here is indeed overcome by such feeling. John's refusal of her advances leaves her 'cut off from those who surrounded her by an emotion which they did not share' (p.173).

While John initially helped Bernard gain fame, he now is the cause of his disgrace, refusing to attend a party where he was to feature as an exotic object. Bernard's reaction to his fall from grace once again shows how childish he is, and he lashes out enviously at the happiness of others, 'revenging himself on [Helmholtz and John] for liking one another more than they liked him' (p.183). Helmholtz shows that he is a person who can truly tolerate the difficulties of the world without cowardly retreating to a *soma* holiday. As a writer he longs for the kind of 'madness and violence' about which Shakespeare was able to write (p.185).

In this chapter we begin to see that rather than being an unfeeling tyrant addicted to power, the World Controller Mustapha Mond thinks he has the best interests of his society at heart. Though his decision to suppress the academic essay is a cowardly act of censorship, he feels it is a means to an end. He knows it is a 'masterly piece of work', but also knows that it 'might easily decondition the more unsettled minds' (p.177). Mond seems almost bored of this way of things, yet is pressured by his job's responsibilities into always enforcing the official view: '"What fun it would be," he [thinks], "if one didn't have to think about happiness!"' (p.142).

Key point

Now that he is in London, John is referred to almost exclusively as the 'Savage', reflecting the way others view him as an exotic and strange 'beast' rather than a human.

Q Why has John grown so unhappy?

Q Can Mustapha Mond's censorship of the article be justified?

Chapter Thirteen

Summary: *Lenina grows increasingly frustrated about her unrequited lust for John; John confesses his love for Lenina but then flies into a 'Shakespearean' rage as Lenina makes sexual advances.*

In a lapse of concentration symbolic of the incompatibility of emotion and social stability, Lenina makes a mistake at her job at the Embryo Store – an error that twenty-two years into the future will have dire consequences, causing 'a promising young Alpha-Minus' to die of a preventable disease (p.187). Lenina is experiencing the 'horrible' condition of postponed gratification described earlier in the book. The thought of delaying sex for emotional reasons is ridiculous to her, and the idea of lifelong monogamy as John clumsily proposes is repulsive. Lenina sneers at the 'savage' conditions he places on their 'love', and attempts to force herself on John sexually.

John turns violent, and quotes Shakespeare (mainly *The Tempest* and *Othello* in this chapter) in order to affirm his beliefs; Lenina quotes *her* 'poetry', repeating hypnopaedic slogans to try and convince John that what she wants to do is right. What Huxley is trying to show, however, is that perhaps *neither* are right: both are, in a way, just appealing to the ideas, opinions and behaviours with which they have been conditioned. While it is easy to see the results of Lenina's hypnopaedic conditioning, Huxley may be suggesting that John has been conditioned by the profound violence inherent in Shakespeare, along with the violence of his upbringing on the reservation. In his fury at Lenina, John acts like Popé and speaks like Othello.

Key point

The scene that unravels between Lenina and John is an example of a typical clash of cultures. Lenina can't understand why John won't have sex with her; John can't understand why Lenina wants to do so without first making him prove his worth.

Q Is the novel suggesting that all feelings are the result of conditioning, or does it elsewhere show that there are natural desires and impulses?

Chapter Fourteen

Summary: John visits Linda in the Park Lane Hospital; Linda dies.

With Linda dying in a hospital bed, John tries to focus on fond memories, but can't keep his rage at her relationship with Popé under control. Once again we see John as a character torn between extremes: the nostalgic memories of growing up with his mother battle with the violent hate he feels toward her for giving herself up to Popé, an act he feels signifies her betrayal of him (Huxley here is dramatising a classic Oedipal Complex [see Background & Context]). When Linda wakes up and mistakes John for her old lover it only makes the situation worse. Huxley seems to suggest that John kills Linda by interrupting her *soma* trip and shaking her. In the middle of a sentence Linda's 'voice suddenly died into an almost inaudible breathless croaking' (p.205). John is driven to a wild despair and withdraws from the world around him: 'in silence he [rises] to his feet, in silence slowly walk[s] towards the door' (p.207). It's clear that he can no longer stand to be part of this civilisation.

Q Why is John so angry towards Linda?

Q What is it about the Bokanovsky twins that John abhors?

Chapter Fifteen

Summary: John causes a riot at the hospital by throwing soma rations out a window; Helmholtz steps in to fight alongside John while Bernard is too indecisive to act.

As he had in the previous chapter, John views a group of Bokanovsky twins as maggots: 'maggots again, but larger, full-grown, they now crawled across his grief and his repentance'. Overcome by this 'nightmare of swarming indistinguishable sameness', he again quotes lines from *The Tempest*. Compared to their earlier appearance, where they were proclaimed in earnest excitement, they are now intended only to note a painful irony: '"How many goodly creatures are there here!" The singing words mocked him derisively. "How beauteous mankind is! O brave new world..."' (p.209). John now feels exactly the opposite to the excitement he felt before coming to London and the hopeful sentiment of these words seems only to mock him like a cruel joke.

But then it all changes: he starts to interpret 'O brave new world' as a 'call to arms' (p.210), and so he seizes the *soma* box and throws the pills out the window. Of all the disruptions John has caused (either directly or indirectly), this is the largest, and indeed inspires a veritable riot against his actions. Helmholtz Watson is inspired by John's example and fights alongside him, showing that he truly is an individual not content with the status quo. Bernard, on the other hand, can only cowardly equivocate. His bout of indecisiveness is a perfect symbol for Bernard as a character. All along he has been pulled and pushed about by different expectations and social pressures, and in the end can only become stuck in this hilariously pathetic indecision. He thinks he wants to be 'different' but is too scared to do what it truly takes.

Q Can some of John's unhappiness be explained by his disappointment at what he thought this world would be? Is his anger a kind of tantrum due to unmet expectations?

Q Why has Huxley chosen Bernard as one of the main characters, instead of Helmholtz who seems much more like a conventional 'hero'?

Chapter Sixteen

Summary: *John, Bernard and Helmholtz are taken to Mustapha Mond's study; Bernard tries to lay the blame on John and Helmholtz and is escorted, in tears, from the room; Mond describes the island to which they are to be sent.*

Mond argues passionately that the society of Brave New World was developed in order to stop the reappearance of war and other human tragedies. He thinks that 'truth and beauty' are merely distractions and that a tragedy like Othello makes no sense in a peaceful society. For him, a stable society where everyone is happy is more important than anything else. Mond also reveals that he was once like Helmholtz and John, someone interested in truth and science, an 'inquisitive young scullion' (pp.225–26). When he was threatened with exile, however, he chose the pathway to leadership over his intellectual pursuits. He does sometimes regret the decision, and is envious of the life that awaits Helmholtz at the island to which other free-thinkers are sent. In the end he believes that the happiness of the masses is more important than his own.

Key point

The island to which Helmholtz and Bernard are to be sent is perhaps the real utopia of the novel, and Mond almost goes so far as to acknowledge this with his envy. By being envious of the life that awaits them, he tacitly admits that the city of London is really just a 'nanny-state' and there are greater joys to be had on the island of free-thinkers.

Q Is Mond convincing when he talks about the need to preserve the peacefulness and happiness of society?

Chapter Seventeen

Summary: Mustapha Mond continues to speak with John; John argues that there can be no true happiness without hardship and pain; he claims the right to be unhappy.

The discussion about the legitimacy of this society continues, with John arguing passionately for what he believes is humankind's natural religious impulse. Unsurprisingly, Mustapha Mond believes that nothing is 'natural' to a human, that all instinct is the result of some form of nurture, that 'one believes things because one has been conditioned to believe them' (pp.234–35). Huxley is involving us in a complex philosophical question: are humans only what they are raised to be, or do they have a true 'essence' that can't be corrupted?

John feels that although Mond's society has eradicated pain and hardship, it has left its citizens with nothing in place of these things. For John, experiencing the bad is necessary if one is to feel the good. It is part of life; the lows are as essential to humankind as the highs. Without the unhappiness and struggle, John feels, we lose a lot of what we consider to be human – the ambition, the bravery, the heroism, the beauty of writers like Shakespeare who speak to the collective struggle of our lives. In 'claiming the right to be unhappy' (p.240), John makes a stand for what he believes is the essence of humanity.

Mustapha Mond claims that John only feels this way because he has grown up in a world based on hardship, and he doesn't think it is right for him to argue against a world he doesn't understand.

Q Does John have a right to object to this society that he doesn't understand?

Q Are pain and unhappiness essential to 'human experience' as John claims?

Chapter Eighteen

Summary: *Helmholtz and Bernard are exiled; John flees to the lighthouse to live in solitude; a wildlife photographer films him and the resultant movie brings hordes of tourists to the lighthouse; overwhelmed with conflicting emotions, John commits suicide.*

John flees to an abandoned lighthouse outside London, where, in complete solitude, he begins to try and cleanse himself of the traces of the 'brave new world'. He prays to all the Gods he knows, crying '"forgive me! Oh make me pure! Oh, help me to be good!" again and again, till he was on the point of fainting from the pain' (p.244). He tries to get back to his past, reliving his life in Malpais, making arrows and spears. He tries to condition himself out his love for Lenina by jumping into a 'clump of hoary juniper bushes' and whipping himself (p.252).

In the meantime, a big-game photographer named Darwin Bonaparte has started to film John's strange behaviour in order to make a 'feely'. The film, depicting John as a wild beast, is a huge success and eventually brings tourists to gawk at him. They throw him peanuts and gum 'as to an ape' (p.255) and demand that John demonstrate his use of the whip upon himself. He eventually gives in and starts whipping himself and a young woman (possibly Lenina) in a frenzy. John is driven to such a state that he succumbs to the gawkers' *soma*-induced 'orgy-porgy'. The guilt in the morning is too much for him and he commits suicide, hanging himself in the lighthouse.

Q Why do the gawkers see John as a wild animal?

Q What, in the end, drives John to suicide?

CHARACTERS & RELATIONSHIPS

John the 'Savage'

Key quote

'But I don't want comfort. I want God, I want poetry, I want real danger, I want freedom, I want goodness. I want sin.' (p.240)

John, the son of Linda and DHC Tomakin, grew up in a Reservation at Malpais, Mexico. A very complicated character, John is caught between conflicting inner extremes in much the same way as he is caught between the two worlds of civilisation and nature. He is an outsider in both Malpais and London. In Malpais people taunt him about his white hair and exclude him from rituals; in London they are fascinated by his strange appearance and beliefs and treat him as though he were an exotic animal. He doesn't feel at home anywhere and would rather just be left alone. In the end he chooses 'the right to be unhappy' (p.240) and sends himself into isolation – the only place he feels at home.

John was raised in a world with social customs that seem more similar to our own than those of London, so we are naturally inclined to identify with the frustration and alienation he feels there. The extremity and violence of his passions, however, also distances him from us. He is a difficult character to identify with, and while he is one of the only characters to raise a serious moral objection to the beliefs of the society, finding its lack of individual freedom deplorable, he seems too unstable and violently irrational for us to view him as a hero.

He is often used by Huxley to symbolise the return of nature and instability to the civilisation of London. For instance, he was born because mankind's power over nature was not complete (Linda's contraceptive device failed), and his presence in London frequently threatens to disrupt the society's strict order. He indirectly makes a worker knock over 'test-tubes of spermatozoa' (p.151), a symbol for the artificial control of life, and his presence distracts Lenina from her job, leading to a grave error. That all of 'upper-caste London was wild to see this delicious creature' (p.153) suggests he has inspired an intensity of emotion that the civilisation has worked hard to eradicate – an intensity which seems natural to humanity. John is also the only person in London to have a mother and father.

John's most important relationship is with Lenina Crowne, whom he loves but at times despises as a 'whore'. For John, Lenina is a symbol of the 'brave new world' and this explains why he holds such conflicting feelings for her. He is fascinated by her perfume, which makes 'his heart beat wildly'; her clothes make him 'enchanted' (p.143), and he obsesses over her beauty like Romeo over Juliet. But his love for her also makes him despise himself. If he loves Lenina, he then thinks it implies that he loves the world of London – a world he holds responsible for the death of his mother Linda. So eventually John comes to hate his desire for Lenina and even sets about trying to condition himself against feeling love and lust for her. Along with whipping himself he leaps into a bush of thorns: '[a]t the edge of the heath stood a clump of hoary juniper bushes. He flung himself against them, he embraced, not the smooth body of his desires, but an armful of green spikes' (p.252).

John detests Lenina's promiscuity, as well as the promiscuity in London society as a whole, although it is conditioned and sanctioned by everyone except him. This is the central dilemma of their relationship. Promiscuity is a cornerstone of social conduct in London, while in Malpais, as in Shakespeare, it is a profound crime to be punished with violence: the two extremes are proven to be irreconcilable in the course of the book's plot. To enjoy life and experience pleasure, for John, is to tacitly agree to the principles of London; self-flagellation represents his attempts to transcend this world. This aspect of his relationship with Lenina also exposes a contradiction within his character: while he rails against what he feels is unnatural about the civilisation in London, he does not let himself act upon his own natural urges. He feels he has to control himself and restrict his impulses.

John also has a strong relationship with Helmholtz Watson. Upon meeting they become instant companions and feel they are kindred spirits who share a belief in the importance of truth and individuality, as well as the power of art and great writing. While Helmholtz cannot understand all of John's 'strange' beliefs, he does appreciate his passion and fights alongside him in his *soma* revolt.

Bernard Marx

Key quotes

'"I am I, and wish I wasn't"; his self-consciousness was acute and distressing.' (p.64)

'A chronic fear of being slighted made him avoid his equals ...' (p.65)

Of all the characters in *Brave New World*, Bernard Marx is the least certain of himself, and is regarded by others as an outsider both physically and mentally. There's a rumour circulating throughout London that 'somebody made a mistake when he was still in the bottle – thought he was a Gamma and put alcohol into his blood-surrogate' (p.46); people use this rumour to account for his shortness and his strange personality. Bernard has an 'unsavoury reputation' because 'he spends most of his time by himself' (p.45) and does not seem to like the things everyone else does. When we first meet him in Chapter Three this description indeed seems accurate. We see him filled with anger about the way Henry Foster speaks about Lenina 'as though she were a bit of meat' (p.45). He is unwilling to conform to what is expected of him, and rather than being continually happy he walks with 'eyes for the most part downcast' (p.63).

In the early parts of the book, we might even begin to think that Bernard is being shaped as the hero of the novel. We are used to a hero being someone unsatisfied with the way a world is, who registers a moral objection and strives to do something about it. But we also begin to see that Bernard is perhaps just bitterly unhappy and extremely self-conscious about his physical 'defects':

> [h]e stood eight centimetres short of the standard Alpha height and was slender in proportion. Contact with members of the lower castes always reminded him painfully of this physical inadequacy (p.64).

The anger that he feels toward those around him, even to the cheerful Benito Hoover, is not necessarily a distaste for the way they behave so much as envy: 'how bitterly he envied men like Henry Foster and Benito Hoover' (p.65). More than anything, Bernard feels 'alien and alone' (p.65) and this, in turn, affects his feelings for others and the world in which he lives. If he feels like an outsider, then he can't help but act like one.

As the novel continues we begin to see that far from being heroic, Bernard is actually quite pathetic and weak. Most of the time he is posturing and posing, pretending to be brave in order to gain attention. At the reservation with Lenina, for example, he goes 'out of his way to show himself strong and unorthodox'. We also see that he is spiteful and petty. While he claims that in John he has found another outsider he can identify with, the real reason he wants to bring him back to London is to get revenge on the Director who has threatened to exile him. Though John's presence in London gains Bernard a certain amount of fame by association, this quickly disappears and Bernard finds himself once again an 'outsider'. Nothing works out for him in the end.

Ultimately, Bernard is someone caught between conflicting desires: a wish to be different but a fear of getting hurt; a desire to be alone but a deep need to fit in. He is a man pushed back and forth by social expectations and crippled by self-consciousness. Far from being a hero, in the end, as he falls to his knees and tries to blame all his problems on others (p.226), he is revealed to be a tragically pathetic character.

Key scene

Perhaps Bernard's defining moment as a character comes during the riot that John causes when he throws rations of *soma* out of a window. John is attacked and Helmholtz Watson runs to his aid. Bernard's actions are very different: he 'ran forward to help them; then thought better of it and halted; then, ashamed, stepped forward again; then again thought better of it, and was standing in an agony of humiliated indecision' (p.214).

Lenina Crowne

Key quotes

'... she's a splendid girl. Wonderfully pneumatic.' (p.44)

'"Somehow," she mused, "I hadn't been feeling very keen on promiscuity lately."' (p.43)

Lenina works in the Embryo Store and is generally a cheerful character who enjoys comfort and safety. Like most of the main characters, we first see Lenina as slightly dissatisfied with her present existence, a little tired with doing what is expected, for example, in the area of promiscuity (p.43). By the end we see her as too scared to be an individual; she is most comfortable conforming to society's expectations, and only flirts with the idea of being different.

Lenina's most significant relationship is with John the Savage, and he causes a pronounced change within her. Early on it is suggested she is naturally attracted to people (like Bernard) who seem different (p.46), and so after John's arrival in London it is not surprising that she quickly grows infatuated with him. But it is hard to tell exactly why she feels such a deep attraction: perhaps it is because John is a fascinating 'spectacle', or perhaps it is because he seems determined not to return her affections and so she pursues him stubbornly. Perhaps it is because John symbolises all the things she wishes she had the courage to be. Either way, he stirs up deep feelings within her. His declarations of love make her blush in an 'emblem of the inner tide of startled elation' she otherwise never expresses (p.191). But this feeling soon turns to horror when John flies into a murderous rage and she runs terrified into the bathroom.

At the end of the novel John is visited at the lighthouse by a young woman with a 'doll-beautiful' face – most probably Lenina, though Huxley doesn't technically identify her as such. She throws her arms out to John, with horrific consequences – riled up by the crowd, John beats her and himself with the whip, participates in an orgy, and commits suicide the next morning.

Helmholtz Watson

Key quotes

'He was a powerfully built man, deep-chested, broad shouldered, massive, and yet quick in his movements, springy and agile.' (p.66)

'A mental excess had produced in Helmholtz Watson effects very similar to those which, in Bernard, were the result of a physical defect.' (p.62)

From the outside, Helmholtz looks like a model citizen. He is a 'powerfully built man' (p.61) and women constantly chase him. He is a successful lecturer at the College of Emotional Engineering and a popular writer of 'feelies' and hypnopaedic rhymes. This 'excess of ability', however, has also made him an outsider. His immense intelligence means he cannot be satisfied doing only what society wants of him. He needs something more and has a wish to write 'something important', something 'intense, more violent' (p.70), but doesn't know what this is, and he is still too much a product of his society to be able to articulate his desire for difference.

Helmholtz is the closest to what we might call a 'hero' in *Brave New World*. While he doesn't achieve all that much with his actions, he remains true to his inner integrity and never sells himself out like the cowardly Bernard. In many ways Helmholtz is the opposite of Bernard. Compared to Bernard's diminutive stature he is tall and strong, and his popularity with women makes Bernard jealous. Helmholtz at first values their friendship because he initially feels that in Bernard he has found someone else who is an outsider, but he eventually comes to see how petty Bernard truly is.

Upon meeting, Helmholtz and John are immediately drawn to each other and become great friends. Helmholtz recognises in John another true individual and is inspired to fight alongside him in his *soma* rebellion, risking punishment and exile.

Mustapha Mond

Key quote

'That's how I paid. By choosing to serve happiness. Other people's – not mine.' (p.229)

Mustapha Mond is the Resident World Controller for Western Europe – an extremely high position of authority. Reflecting this social standing he always walks 'briskly' and speaks with the utmost confidence and self-assurance; others react to him with great deference. A mere 'look from Mustapha Mond' reduces Bernard 'to an abject silence' (p.218), and his voice is 'a trumpet' (p.42).

At first, Mond seems to be a firm but somehow likable figure – not a hard-line dictator like Joseph Stalin. He is cultured, erudite, inquisitive, fatherly – but these are all characteristics he denies to anyone else in the society, just as he denies them access to the intellectual works he so enjoys. He sits in judgment over others with an impunity that even Stalin might have envied. When Helmholtz says 'It's more like a caffeine-solution party than a trial', Huxley is drawing attention to the fact that their interview with Mond *is* a trial, one every bit as arbitrary as the show trials of the Soviet Union. Where Stalin was the embodiment of an authoritarian system that relied on terror, Mond is the embodiment of one in which people are made to 'love their servitude'. He makes it all seem necessary and satisfactory, even harmonious, but it is no less the authoritarian 'nightmare' (as Huxley calls it in his letter to George Orwell) than Stalin's Soviet Union. Yet it is easy to be beguiled by Huxley's portrait of this 'kindly' father-figure, who is a little regretful that he has had to sacrifice his own ambitions to guide his Utopia.

The Director/ DHC/ Tomakin

Key quotes

'He had a long chin and big, rather prominent teeth, just covered, when he was not talking, by his full, floridly curved lips.' (p.4)

'Pale, wild-eyed, the Director glared about him in an agony of bewildered humiliation' (p.152)

The Director of Hatcheries and Conditioning is, like Mustapha Mond, a man of great authority, but he lacks the confidence and poise of the World Controller. On the tour with the students at the start of the novel, he spruiks the society's philosophies proudly, almost cockily, and speaks 'triumphantly' as he watches the children in the nursery being conditioned by electric shocks. But when he notices the presence of Mustapha Mond he is visibly rattled, almost becoming nervous. He 'sprang to his feet' and smiled 'with all his teeth, effusive' (p.33) as if he were desperate to please his superior.

The Director is John's father, but did not know of his existence until John arrived in London. He had been on a date with John's mother Linda in Malpais when a storm separated them, losing Linda (he thought) to the wilderness, and leaving the fact of Linda's pregnancy unknown to him. Upon John's return to London he is overcome with embarrassment and shamed into resigning his position.

Linda

Key quote

'The return to civilisation was for her the return to *soma*, was the possibility of lying in bed and taking holiday after holiday ...' (p.154).

Linda is the mother of John and was once a citizen of London before she became lost in a storm while on a trip to Malpais with the Director. While raising John in the Reservation, Linda often told him stories of London, making it seem like a utopian wonderland. Upon her return she is so glad to be back that she loses herself on an extended *soma* 'holiday' and eventually dies. Either way, her fall into *soma* represents her relief at being free once more from the hardships of life in the Reservation. Unlike John it seems she never grew to love 'native' life. Unlike her son, Linda was conditioned from infancy and is unable to overcome her revulsion for the reservation's characteristics.

THEMES, IDEAS AND VALUES

Nature vs nurture

Key quotes

'As if one believed anything by instinct! One believes things because one has been conditioned to believe them.' (p.234)

'The students nodded, emphatically agreeing with a statement which upwards of sixty-two thousand repetitions in the dark had made them accept, not merely as true, but as axiomatic, self-evident, utterly indisputable.' (p.40)

'An emblem of the inner tide of startled elation, the blood rushed up into Lenina's cheeks.' (p.191)

One of the most important themes in *Brave New World* is the division between nature and nurture, or what can be considered natural and instinctual to humankind and what is learned or cultured. The book challenges our own definitions of these concepts and frequently makes us consider the way traits we thought natural and innate might instead be the result of learning and conditioning. It also asks us to do the opposite, to argue against people like Mustapha Mond who promote the view that '[p]rovidence takes its cue from men' (p.236), that humankind can create any world it wants for itself and is free of the burdens and chains of instinct.

The debate between nature and nurture has a long history in both philosophy and psychology. It is an important argument, because whether we decide we are wholly natural organisms or are substantially created and cultured will determine how we view ourselves, as well as the actions and beliefs of people from different cultures. For example, if we believe that humans are naturally monogamous, we are likely to view people from polygamist and promiscuous societies like the one in *Brave New World* as unnatural and strange. This kind of thinking is a dangerous practice and can ultimately lead to such ugly things as racism and xenophobia.

On the other hand, if we believe that all our values and beliefs are due to nurture – what we have learnt and been taught by our cultural environment – and that what we think is right and good and true depends entirely on how we were raised and 'conditioned', then we might find it difficult to argue against other people's behaviour that seems wrong to us. If anything goes, if (as Mustapha Mond claims) one 'believes things because one has been conditioned to believe them' (p.234), then it seems to imply that truth and a sense of right and wrong are only created products with no stable essence.

Clearly, neither viewpoint seems entirely satisfactory – both have benefits and drawbacks. *Brave New World* argues against adopting either extreme position and instead encourages us to view humankind as the product of equal parts nature and nurture. While there are many examples in the novel of the efficacy of conditioning in creating beliefs and behaviours, there are just as many which speak to a set of natural needs, desires and reactions common to humankind that cannot be entirely overcome.

Examples of nurture

The use of hypnopaedia and other forms of conditioning show to what extent this society relies on the power of culture to construct beliefs and feelings. In the Infant Nurseries, loudspeakers whisper lessons on 'Elementary Class Consciousness' and 'Elementary Sex' (p.27). Characters frequently recite rhymes and hypnopaedic slogans whenever they start to doubt their world, and hypnopaedia is considered the 'greatest moralising and socialising force of all time' (p.28), ensuring that the society functions as it does. Throughout the novel we're given frequent examples of how efficacious this conditioning has been in encouraging people to follow constructed beliefs and behaviours as if they were indeed natural, and to some degree this confirms the belief in the power of nurture over nature.

One of the interesting ideas of the book is that John's frequent recitation of passages from Shakespeare also represents a kind of conditioning, and so even the supposedly most 'natural' individual appears as the product of cultural conditioning too. John is often presented as a figure representing nature, but many of his beliefs are arguably just as constructed and nurtured as those of the citizens of London. While other characters have learnt phrases and rhymes in order to reinforce their beliefs and actions, John uses quotations from *Romeo and Juliet, Othello* and *Hamlet* in order to understand situations and make decisions, and his view of what is natural to humankind is a very Shakespearean one. His usage of Shakespearean quotes, however, is often decontextualised. This may be intended to cast a slightly satirical light on the readers who have, like John, grown up in a world in love with authors like Shakespeare. Perhaps we're just as conditioned as he? It could also be argued that John has been 'conditioned' by the social mores of Malpais.

Examples of nature

Despite the many examples of the effectiveness of conditioning (or nurture), there are still just as many – albeit more subtle – instances of a shared nature between humans. While conditioning has definitely worked in the society of London, the city is still haunted by the presence of many natural urges and impulses. The fact that the society is so strict about its policies of conditioning and so wary of the influence of outsiders and different opinions (shown best by Mustapha Mond's suppression of a scientific article on p.177) shows that they recognise that there *is* an innate human nature that can upset the strict order if left unchecked, a nature that must be controlled. In many ways London exists in a state of constant fear of the return of nature, because nature represents the forces of instability (an instability which might otherwise be called freedom). If Mond truly believes that all man's beliefs are derived from nurture, then there would be no reason to condition them so extensively. He fears that the old 'tyrannies' such as family and Christianity will undo the citizens' conditioning.

The insistence on control and conditioning belies this belief that humankind is dominated by nurture rather than nature. That a person like Lenina can feel the strong emotions she does for John, despite the fact she has been brought up not to have them, shows that they are still naturally possible and that all our morals and emotions are not truly constructed by culture. Indeed, the best place to see the way the natural still persists is within the Alpha classes, who are still 'capable (within limits) of making a free choice' (p.222). The way these natural feelings most often manifest is in moments of unhappiness. For example, Lenina frequently hovers on the edge of the realisation that she does not agree with the principles of Society. Similarly, Helmholtz Watson wants to do 'something much more important' (p.70) with his writing than the simple hypnopaedic rhymes he composes. Neither character is content to conform to the status quo, and in this dissatisfaction we can discern the presence of their natural humanity – a humanity that is not able to be conditioned to feel what its government wants it to feel.

Freedom and control

Key quote

'When the individual feels, the community reels' (p.94)

'There was a choice between World Control and destruction' (p.48)

The most obvious thing missing in the society of London is freedom, and it is what its rulers fear the most. Interestingly, there are no great external restrictions to freedom – no policemen lining the streets forcing people to behave a certain way. As Huxley wrote in a letter to George Orwell, 'the lust for power can be just as completely satisfied by suggesting people into loving their servitude as by flogging and kicking them into obedience' (quoted in Baker 1990, p.23). The reason why the control of society is so effective is that the control of freedom is internalised: because they have all been brainwashed, the citizens restrict themselves. Every time a character begins to feel a little uncertain about their life and longs for the ability to decide something on their own, they remember the hypnopaedic rhymes that stand in the way of free thought and convince them that all is well, that they don't need anything else. For example, when we first are introduced to Lenina we can see that she is a little dissatisfied with her current life. She doesn't want to keep dating a whole range of different people and feels content just to keep seeing Henry Foster. She says to her friend Fanny that she '"hadn't been feeling very keen on promiscuity lately. There are times when one doesn't"'. But soon after she remembers one of the hypnopaedic slogans, 'everyone belongs to everyone else' (p.45). These slogans reinforce the ideology of the society and represent internalised mechanisms of control. The greatest lack of freedom is the inability to think freely, and indeed this is the case for nearly everyone in *Brave New World*.

Everyone is subject to the control of thought, yet the lower classes like the Epsilon Semi-Morons are also the victims of biological restrictions.

While these lower classes are physically and mentally engineered to be content with their banal lives, this does not excuse the fact they are essentially bred to be slaves of the higher classes, to do all the jobs the Alphas do not want to do themselves. So while it might be true that the Epsilons 'don't really mind being Epsilons' (p.67), the fact that they are only there to support the luxurious lives of the upper classes is decidedly unfair. That they are deliberately tampered with by genetic modification and made to be less capable than others is not a 'great' act that allows for social stability: it is the breeding of slaves.

At one point John asks Mustapha why everyone is not engineered to be an Alpha-Double-Plus, to which he replies '[b]ecause we have no wish to have our throats cut' (p.222). So while he claims the subjugation of the lower classes enables stability and peace, from another angle we can see that Mustapha's justification exposes the selfishness of the upper classes. They breed the Epsilons so life for them (the Alphas) can be stable and enjoyable and so that they do not have to tolerate social unrest or the unhappiness that an Alpha would feel performing repetitive manual labour. But just because the lower classes are 'happy' does not override the fact that they are being deliberately deprived of the possibility of individual freedom. While in our own world many people indeed do live lives similar to those of the Deltas and Epsilons, working repetitive jobs with no larger life goals, at least they have the possibility of choosing not to do this. It is this potential for freedom which makes all the difference, and the thing that is lacking for the lower castes.

Freedom from unhappiness?

Against all these alleged abuses, Mustapha Mond would argue that the lack of freedom upon which the society is based actually enables a different kind of freedom: freedom from unhappiness. For him, the control of individual thought and behaviour grants a larger and more important type of liberation – the freedom from hardship and pain. Mond believes that the strict ordering of society is worth more than individual freedom because it ultimately avoids such things as war: '[w]hat's the point of truth or beauty or knowledge when the anthrax bombs are popping all around you?' (p.228). So, rather than freedom, stability is instead 'the primal and the ultimate need' (p.43) that must be secured at all costs, because otherwise the world descends into chaos. Obviously, this invokes a different sense of the word 'freedom' than we ordinarily associate it with, but it is still technically correct: it means the freedom not to be dominated by hardship, and in many ways this is the goal of many of our current societies. While in the novel a large aspect of individual life is strictly controlled, a citizen of the 'brave new world' does not have to worry about anxiety, sadness, pain, hunger, hardship or woe: '[n]o pains have been spared to make ... lives emotionally easy' (p.45). For Mond there 'isn't any need for a civilised man to bear anything that's seriously unpleasant' (p.236), and because of this he would argue that there is no need for individual freedom. If a person is purely happy, what could they need freedom for? What is freedom except the freedom to cause oneself sadness and woe? Or, as he says to John, 'the right to be unhappy' (p.240). Mond actually thinks the forms of freedom we are used to in our own world only represent the freedom to be 'miserable': 'There was something called liberalism ... speeches about liberty of the subject. Liberty to be inefficient and miserable. Freedom to be a round peg in a square hole' (p.46).

What Mond neglects, however, is that often just the experience of individual freedom is itself a source of great happiness. Indeed, John argues passionately that one cannot truly be happy if one doesn't have freedom, including the freedom to experience pain and hardship. For him, happiness is meaningless without the lows of sadness. Without pain and hardship happiness just becomes the norm and so becomes no great thing at all. To be able to be happy one needs to be able to *choose* happiness, or in John's case, unhappiness. John's choice to live a life of pain and solitude, more than anything else, represents his decision to be free.

Difference and discrimination

Key quote

'The ape had spoken ...' (p.255)

In *Brave New World Revisited*, a collection of essays assessing the implications of his novel, Huxley wrote that in the course of evolution 'nature has gone to endless trouble to see that every individual is unlike every other individual':

> Physically and mentally each one of us is unique. Any culture which, in the interests of efficiency or in the name of some political or religious dogma, seeks to standardise the human individual, commits an outrage against man's biological nature. (Huxley 1965, p.36)

The civilisation depicted in *Brave New World* is an example of such a culture, one founded on the eradication of difference. While there are certainly different class divisions, everyone is expected to behave in much the same way and think the same things. Its citizens are often described as 'aphides and ants' (p.63), the city likened to an insect colony with a high level of rigid social organisation.

One of the many effects of this culture is that anyone different is discriminated against. In many ways *Brave New World* is a book about the struggle of outsiders trying to find happiness in a society that will not tolerate their desire to be different. John, Bernard, Helmholtz and (to a lesser extent) Lenina are all hovering on the edges of a society that demands they conform, and even Mustapha Mond was once nearly exiled for his rebellious behaviour. Along with its control of individual freedom, the society's intolerance of difference exposes the crucial ethical flaw at its heart.

The most obvious example of discrimination is the treatment of John. John's arrival in London has a significant impact, and the fact that once he is there the narrator starts referring to him almost exclusively as 'the Savage' reflects the way other people see him. They can't get past his different appearance and behaviours; they have to name him by his difference. The term 'Savage' keeps him at arm's length, like a strange piece of wildlife. The way people think of John only as 'a delicious creature' (p.153) means that, while his strangeness excites them, he will never be understood and accepted by them as anything but a spectacle. The dinner parties organised by Bernard to garner fame by showing John are like carnival freak-shows. Huxley's London may claim to be a place of peace and stability, yet it is incredibly intolerant of a person with different beliefs, and so is only truly peaceful for its own inhabitants.

The final chapter of the book, set at the lighthouse where John has exiled himself, best shows how little these people regard John as an actual person. Darwin Bonaparte, the 'Feely Corporation's most expert big-game photographer', films John as though he were an elephant or a gorilla. Indeed, Bonaparte expects his film to be as successful as another of his called the 'Sperm Whale's Love-Life' (p.253). The tourists who come to gawk at him throw peanuts, 'as to an ape', and when John talks it is as if the 'ape had spoken' (p.255).

By not being able to accommodate or accept his different feelings and beliefs, the people of London indirectly drive John to his death. At first, before leaving Malpais, he was incredibly excited by the prospect of coming to this 'brave new world', but he soon loses his enthusiasm once he realises he can only once again be treated as an outsider: 'At Malpais he had suffered because they had shut him out from the communal activities of the pueblo, in civilised London he was suffering because he could never escape from those communal activities, never be quietly alone' (p.235).

While Huxley definitely intends the citizens of London to be the worst exponents of this discriminatory behaviour, he does show that it also happens at the Reservation in Malpais. Whilst growing up in Malpais John was excluded from the rituals and customs of the indigenous people because he had 'white hair' and was not of indigenous birth. He tells Bernard that the others 'shut me out of absolutely everything', and at one point he was pelted with 'a shower of stones' and driven into isolation (p.136).

Despite constantly being treated as an outsider, John does much the same thing to other people. He refuses to understand what he considers to be the strange customs of London and lashes out violently at Lenina for her different beliefs in regards to sexuality. He is almost as guilty of practicing discrimination, as intolerant of people who seem different, than those who label him a 'savage' and an 'ape'.

It is clear that Huxley, by making all sides potentially guilty of discrimination, is suggesting that discrimination is to some degree a natural tendency of humanity, but something we should work to control and overcome. It is perhaps natural that humans are attracted to or scared of things that seem different and strange. They grab our attention, and in our own lives we frequently gaze upon different cultures and behaviours with a degree of fascination not terribly dissimilar to the kind exhibited by the 'tourists' in the closing scenes of *Brave New World*. But what Huxley tries to show is that regarding someone with a view only towards their difference does them a great injustice. It most frequently leads to ostracism. At worst it can lead to racism and xenophobia. In *Brave New World* the society may have immense inner stability, but conditioned hatred and suspicion exists between castes. Nor can the Londoners accept John due to his different behaviour. It cannot be considered an ethical or moral civilisation for this reason.

Happiness or humanity?

Key quotes

'"And do remember that a gramme is better than a damn."' (p.55)

'"What fun it would be," he thought, "if one didn't have to think about happiness!"' (p.177)

'Actual happiness always looks pretty squalid in comparison with the over-compensation for misery' (p.221)

Brave New World forces us to ask what price we put on happiness, and also questions the very nature of this emotion.

In our everyday lives, we frequently strive to achieve comfort and pleasure, and the reason we go to school and work and do things that are hard and laborious is so that eventually, in the future, we might obtain happiness. The underlying utopian promise of many advertisements, government policies, films and books is that we should strive towards a world where everything is purely good, where we only have to experience pleasure and comfort and none of the negative emotions. But what if all this came true? *Brave New World* forces us to consider this question.

From one perspective, the society in *Brave New World* is an example of a utopian drive for permanent happiness gone too far. In its quest for a life of pure happiness it has eradicated all those things that our culture considers unique to 'humanity': creativity, freedom, ambition, passion, intensity, curiosity and the life of the mind. While there are some benefits, such as medical care and sexual liberation, these seem to be outweighed by the absence of things that make happiness a special kind of emotion. In John's opinion the kind of happiness that pervades the society is not happiness at all, but just a kind of numbness. He believes we need struggle and pain and hardship if happiness is to have any meaning in itself. It is not an emotion with an autonomous identity; it only grows substance in opposition to the negative emotions, and is defined against these.

The novel's treatment of happiness is intended to make us reflect on how in our own lives we tend to become overly invested in utopian ideals. If this is a society where happiness is supposedly all that everyone feels, but is really just a dull and lifeless place, then it can make us question the many little complaints we make as well as the great stock we put towards achieving a 'better life'. For if we learn that '[a]ctual happiness always looks pretty squalid in comparison with the over-compensation for misery' (p.221) then we might begin actually to appreciate those other aspects of life that seem opposed to happiness but stand to teach us something. *Brave New World* wants us to consider that perhaps it is not reasonable, as we think it is in our modern world, to expect constant happiness, and that if we actually obtained this it might not be so great after all: it might just be numbness instead.

The kind of happiness promoted by the society can also be seen to represent only one particular kind of happiness – something more like mindless sensual pleasure than complete existential satisfaction. Indeed, this is confirmed by the unrest felt by characters like Helmholtz and Bernard. Despite being told they are living lives of pure happiness, there are definitely things they are dissatisfied with. There are other, more subtle kinds of fulfilment that this society does not cater for and actually tries to stop its citizens feeling. The book wants to show us that happiness can come in many different forms other than immediate pleasure and gratification: there are less easily attainable forms of happiness that we need in order to live a fulfilled existence, forms that cannot be catered to by a magical drug.

Key point

The way it deals with the idea of happiness makes *Brave New World* a unique novel. Many books (and especially Hollywood films) present happiness as the ultimate goal of life and it is the thing towards which their characters strive. Once they have achieved this happiness these narratives end and we are left to think that the characters will go on living 'happily ever after' as in a fairy tale. Huxley's novel refuses to buy into this narrative cliché, however, and his criticism of ideologies of happiness is both a challenge to the way we think about our lives, but also to those many works of narrative art that take it as their final goal. Can one really live a life of complete happiness and still feel happy? Is the 'happily ever after' ending a fairy tale we too often believe?

Brave New World today

To what extent does the world of the novel reflect our own? A reviewer from the *Providence Journal-Bulletin* wrote of *Brave New World:* 'Chilling... That [Huxley] gave us the dark side of genetic engineering in 1932 is amazing'. This is a common reaction to *Brave New World* – readers often comment that Huxley was incredibly far ahead of his time in many respects, and many believe that our 21st-century society is on-course to turn into a similar dystopia. Ideas about genetic manipulation, class distinction, consumerism, technology, sexuality and labour have changed dramatically since 1932, yet they are as pressing now as they were in the 1930s. Think about Huxley's various predictions and whether or not they have come nearer to fruition in the past 80 years.

DIFFERENT INTERPRETATIONS

Different interpretations arise from different responses to a text. Over time, a text will give rise to a wide range of responses from its readers, who may come from various social or cultural groups and live in very different places and historical periods. These responses can be published in newspapers, journals and books by critics and reviewers, or they can be expressed in discussions among readers in the media, classrooms, book groups and so on. While there is no single correct reading or interpretation of a text, it is important to understand that an interpretation is more than a personal opinion – it is the justification of a point of view on the text. To present an interpretation of the text based on your point of view you must use a logical argument and support it with relevant evidence from the text.

Critical viewpoints

Brave New World raises many points upon which critics and readers disagree. The text isn't designed to provide easy answers to the questions it raises; rather it forces a reader to interpret its characters, themes and ideas carefully.

The reception of Huxley's novel has been varied, but the most popular interpretation is that *Brave New World* is a portrait of a dystopian society that thrives on conformity and sameness at the expense of human nature. Upon its publication many critics and reviewers praised its treatment of science and technology, reading the novel as a warning to untamed progress in these fields. The philosopher Bertrand Russell even believed that Huxley's vision of the future was all but inevitable, stating that 'while Mr Huxley's prophecy is meant to be fantastic, it is all too likely to come true' (quoted in Baker 1990, p.15).

Many view the novel as a warning against totalitarian government, and see it as a criticism of all political ideologies based on social planning and control. Jake Pollerd believes that Huxley's chief characters, Bernard Marx, Helmholtz Watson and John the Savage, are all heroic models of civil disobedience, their individuality challenging 'the insipid values the

World State enshrines' (Pollerd 2010, p.89). For many, Huxley's book is about this power of human rebellion.

The book has also generated its fair share of controversy, especially among conservatives who have claimed it promotes scandalous views about marriage, family and sexuality. These kind of knee-jerk reactions are examples of bad reading: anyone who reads the book properly can see that its treatment of these ideas is much more complex and it can hardly be said to unequivocally endorse the beliefs of the society it portrays.

Recent trends in scholarship have also come to pose very different readings of the book. Rather than seeing it as a satirical portrait of a soulless totalitarian government, Joanne Woiak believes that Huxley actually intended his depiction of genetic manipulation and social stratification to be a 'plan for reforming society' (Woiak 2010, p.164). Read in context with Huxley's beliefs and interests at the time, Woiak believes that *Brave New World* reflects:

> ... public anxieties about the supposedly degenerating hereditary quality of the population and how this decline would affect England's economic and political future. For Huxley at this time in his life and in this social context, eugenics was not a nightmare prospect but rather the best hope for designing a better world if used in the right ways by the right people. (Woiak 2010, p.164)

While in later years of his life Huxley would come to repudiate such ideas, at the time of the book's publication he was very interested in the science of eugenics (the attempt to improve a population through selective breeding) and social planning. In the end, Woiak believes that *Brave New World* can be read 'in a relatively optimistic way':

> Oppressive methods – such as compulsory genetic manipulation – had been necessary and tolerable in order to achieve the desired goal of social and economic stability. Rule by meritocracy – the enlightened World Controllers of AF 632 – was the best alternative after democracy had failed. And a stratified and soulless society was a less horrifying scenario than a country exclusively composed of low-functioning Epsilons (2010, p.167).

This recent trend in Huxley criticism attempts to pay close attention to the complex and often contradictory themes and ideas of his novel, and refuses to read *Brave New World* solely as a work of satire.

Two interpretations

1 ***Brave New World* is a warning against uncontrolled advances in science and technology.**

At its core, the future depicted in Huxley's novel is a warning to a capitalist world obsessed with progress at any cost. While the stability allowed for by advances in technology and science has made life idyllic for those at the top, these developments have also allowed for gross abuses of humanity. Those in the lowest rungs of the society are genetically and psychologically bred to be slaves and their ceaseless labour enables the luxurious and hedonistic lives of the selfish Alphas. The upper castes have 'no wish to have [their] throats cut' (p.174) and so the technologies and sciences of genetic manipulation, conditioning and brainwashing have enabled the rulers of this world to create a society which is largely unable to question and rebel against its rule. Hypnopaedia and *soma* have enabled them to erect 'a quite impenetrable wall between the actual universe and [the citizens'] minds' (p.69), and so while everyone claims to be happy, it's impossible to tell if this is truly the case. The fact that none of this mass-conformity would be possible without the technological and scientific advances in the fields of biology, pharmacology and psychology suggests that there is a threshold to which these fields can progress without presenting dangers to society and humanity, especially if they fall into the wrong hands.

2 ***Brave New World* depicts a utopian society that truly cares about its citizens' wellbeing.**

While there are definitely things missing from the society in *Brave New World*, these absences are outweighed by the far greater achievements of stability. By engineering a peaceful and stable society, the leaders of this world have ensured that the great tragedies of the past, the wars and famines that have bloodied our history, will not be repeated. The strict processes of control, while harsh, are means to an end – an end which is ultimately greater than those things lost along the way.

The qualities of humankind which are suppressed in this society and which are often championed in opposition to it, things such as freedom, individuality and creativity, are also revealed in the book to be petty indulgences that are outweighed by more important considerations. Characters like Bernard Marx pretend to want solitude and individuality, but they really just long to fit in. John the Savage violently rebels against the artificial aspects of the society but is shown to practice his own forms of tyranny, lashing out at himself for following his natural urges and beating Lenina for following hers.

The society depicted in Huxley's novel calls the bluff of most nations: we all claim we want peace and happiness, but are ultimately unwilling to make sacrifices in order to achieve these things. It is thus a truly *brave new world* that is willing to make these tough decisions in order to secure safety and happiness for all. Those things it loses do not outweigh the great gains of safety and wellbeing.

QUESTIONS & ANSWERS

This section focuses on your own analytical writing on the text, and gives you strategies for producing high quality responses in your coursework and exam essays.

Essay writing – an overview

An essay is a formal and serious piece of writing that presents your point of view on the text, usually in response to a given essay topic. Your 'point of view' in an essay is your interpretation of the meaning of the text's language, structure, characters, situations and events, supported by detailed analysis of textual evidence.

Analyse – don't summarise

In your essays it is important to avoid simply summarising what happens in a text:

- A **summary** is a description or paraphrase (retelling in different words) of the characters and events. For example: 'Macbeth has a horrifying vision of a dagger dripping with blood before he goes to murder King Duncan'.

- An **analysis** is an explanation of the real meaning or significance that lies 'beneath' the text's words (and images, for a film). For example: 'Macbeth's vision of a bloody dagger shows how deeply uneasy he is about the violent act he is contemplating – as well as his sense that supernatural forces are impelling him to act'.

A limited amount of summary is sometimes necessary to let your reader know which part of the text you wish to discuss. However, always keep this to a minimum and follow it immediately with your analysis (explanation) of what this part of the text is really telling us.

Plan your essay

Carefully plan your essay so that you have a clear idea of what you are going to say. The plan ensures that your ideas flow logically, that your argument remains consistent and that you stay on the topic. An essay plan should be a list of **brief dot points** – no more than half a page. It includes:

- your central argument or main contention – a concise statement (usually in a single sentence) of your overall response to the topic. See 'Analysing a sample topic' for guidelines on how to formulate a main contention.

- three or four dot points for each paragraph indicating the main idea and evidence/examples from the text. Note that in your essay you will need to *expand* on these points and *analyse* the evidence.

Structure your essay

An essay is a complete, self-contained piece of writing. It has a clear beginning (the introduction), middle (several body paragraphs) and end (the last paragraph or conclusion). It must also have a central argument that runs throughout, linking each paragraph to form a coherent whole. See examples of introductions and conclusions in the 'Analysing a sample topic' and 'Sample answer' sections.

The introduction establishes your overall response to the topic. It includes your main contention and outlines the main evidence you will refer to in the course of the essay. Write your introduction *after* you have done a plan and *before* you write the rest of the essay.

The body paragraphs argue your case – they present evidence from the text and explain how this evidence supports your argument. Each body paragraph needs:

- a strong **topic sentence** (usually the first sentence) that states the main point being made in the paragraph

- **evidence** from the text, including some brief quotations

- **analysis** of the textual evidence explaining its significance and explanation of how it supports your argument

- **links back to the topic** in one or more statements, usually towards the end of the paragraph.

Connect the body paragraphs so that your discussion flows smoothly. Use some linking words and phrases like 'similarly' and 'on the other hand', though don't start every paragraph like this. Another strategy is to use a significant word from the last sentence of one paragraph in the first sentence of the next.

Use key terms from the topic – or similes for them – throughout, so the relevance of your discussion to the topic is always clear.

The conclusion ties everything together and finishes the essay. It includes strong statements that emphasise your central argument and provide a clear response to the topic.

Avoid simply restating the points made earlier in the essay – this will end on a very flat note and imply that you have run out of ideas and vocabulary. The conclusion is meant to be a logical extension of what you have written, not just a repetition or summary of it. Writing an effective conclusion can be a challenge. Try using these tips:

- Start by linking back to the final sentence of the second-last paragraph – this helps your writing to 'flow', rather than just leaping back to your main contention straight away.

- Use similes and expressions with equivalent meanings to vary your vocabulary. This allows you to reinforce your line of argument without being repetitive.

- When planning your essay, think of one or two broad statements or observations about the text's wider meaning. These should be related to the topic and your overall argument. Keep them for the conclusion, since they will give you something 'new' to say but still follow logically from your discussion. The introduction will be focused on the topic, but the conclusion can present a wider view of the text.

ESSAY TOPICS

1 "In a properly organised society like ours, nobody has any opportunities for being noble or heroic." Is *Brave New World* a book without a hero?

2 '*Brave New World* argues that social stability is more important than truth'. Discuss.

3 'The disruptive presence of John the Savage shows what an unstable place London really is.' Discuss.

4 'In the end, *Brave New World* is a book that forces us to ask what is more important: community or individuality.' Discuss.

5 "When the individual feels, the community reels". How true is this of the society depicted in *Brave New World*?

6 "One believes things because one has been conditioned to believe them." How is this true of the characters in *Brave New World?*

7 '*Brave New World* is a book that presents two sides to every argument'. Discuss the ways in which the novel presents conflicting portrayals of characters and themes.

8 '*Brave New World* presents a nightmarish vision of the future where happiness has been replaced by mindless pleasure'. Discuss.

9 Is Bernard Marx a jealous and cowardly character, or is he simply misunderstood?

10 'John is a noble individual who fights heroically for freedom'. Discuss.

Vocabulary for writing on *Brave New World*

Totalitarian: A form of government that demands its citizens conform to the rule of the State.

Ostracism: The practice of excluding, banishing or exiling an individual from a community, group or society.

Ambiguous: Able to be understood in more than one way.

Utopia: A place or condition that is perfect, peaceful and harmonious.

Dystopia: A utopia gone wrong, a place or condition in which attempts at peace and harmony create strife and discord.

Analysing a sample topic

"One believes things because one has been conditioned to believe them."
How true is this of the characters in Brave New World?

The first thing to do when analysing an essay topic is to identify the key terms and underlying assumptions. This helps you to provide clear answers to the question and may allow you to think about it in novel and inventive ways.

In this instance, the first part of the topic asks you to identify examples of the things characters believe about life and the world, as well as any examples of how these beliefs have been created artificially rather than arising naturally. Some of the things you might want to consider include the uses of hypnopaedia, the electric shocks that teach the infants to fear beauty, and the many slogans that characters frequently recite, such 'a gramme is better than a damn'. Remember that when identifying the key components it is always useful to already be thinking about ways to support your answer with examples from the text. Start to jot down some ideas and connections.

The next part of the question asks you to evaluate how true the statement is. So while you might find examples that support the statement about the efficacy of conditioning, it is also asking you to do the opposite, to look for examples of beliefs, feelings and behaviours that might have arisen naturally, that might be shared in common amongst humanity and are not the result of conditioning. The question asks you to decide if, within the book, all beliefs really are just the end result of social conditioning – and humanity has no true essence other than what it learns – or if there are actually examples of feelings, opinions and behaviours in the novel that instead seem natural to humanity and so challenge this view. Remember, there are no right or wrong answers; what an essay topic asks you to do is interpret and respond with your own argument supported by evidence from the text.

By looking at all parts of the question like this you are also able to unpack the larger argument underlying the topic. This one is not just asking you to list examples of conditioning, but to enter into a debate about the nature of humankind: are all the things we feel and believe just the result of what we have been taught to believe, or is there an essential and shared nature between humans?

Sample introduction

The rulers of the society in *Brave New World* have employed various forms of conditioning to create what they think is a perfect society. Hypnopaedia, the feelies and extensive processes of brainwashing have enabled the civilisation to create citizens perfectly suited to its goal of social stability. On the surface this all seems to have worked with great efficacy, but there are too many instances of social dissatisfaction for it to be entirely true. Deep down inside many individuals the presence of innate, natural and unconditioned desires constantly threaten to surface. In the mini-rebellions of Helmholtz and Lenina, and in the buried unhappiness of Mustapha Mond's past, we can see that the official belief in conditioning is in the end more hopeful than true, perhaps just another instance of conditioning itself.

First Paragraph

Helmholtz Watson's dissatisfaction with life.

- He wants to write something more important than hypnopaedic slogans, and he is bored with just dating girls and taking *soma*.

- He knows there is something more to life than what is being told to him. He resists the conditioning and forms his own beliefs.

Second Paragraph

Conditioning also fails to account for all of Lenina's beliefs.

- Lenina is moved by John to feel emotions that set her apart from other citizens, emotions that she can't have possibly learnt through conditioning.

- Lenina blushes with deep emotion when around John. She grows distracted at work when pining for him.

- Despite the fact that she has been taught to want many partners, she only wants to be with John. She has been taught to fear intense emotions like love, but John unleashes it within her. Conditioning fails to account for all her beliefs; some of them are natural.

Third Paragraph

Even Mustapha Mond once felt unhappy with the strict order of society and wanted more out of life.

- In the end he chose to uphold the official view but still feels that it might be more fun if one didn't have 'to think about someone else's happiness'.

- He envies Helmholtz and Bernard who are being exiled to the island for free-thinkers.

Fourth Paragraph

All these examples suggest that there is a natural world of emotions beyond those which are conditioned.

- If all beliefs are the result of learning, then where do these intense feelings of dissatisfaction come from? There must be natural desires and beliefs that are deeper than conditioned ones.

- If there is so much unhappiness within the society, then all beliefs cannot be merely the result of conditioning, because these feelings have not been conditioned: they are natural responses and represent the innate and unconditioned beliefs of humankind.

Conclusion

While conditioning has been effective to a degree in controlling the society's citizens, there are much deeper emotions that are constantly threatening to surface. If beliefs are only the result of social learning, entirely due to nurture, than there is no way to explain the presence of the dissatisfaction that characters like Helmholtz, Lenina and even Mustapha Mond feel. Mond's own pronouncement that beliefs are only the end product of conditioning is contradicted by the fact that many characters, including himself, feel restless and uninspired and yearn for 'something more important'. They have never been taught to feel these things, yet still experience them with great urgency. In the end, *Brave New World* suggests that although conditioning has had great influence within its civilisation, there are still just as many natural desires and beliefs waiting to find expression.

SAMPLE ANSWER

'John is a noble individual who fights heroically for freedom.' Discuss.

While there are several characters who think they have society's best interest at heart, John the 'Savage' seems most apt to be labelled heroic. He is constantly positioned as an agent of change, the answer to a steady current of social unrest brewing beneath the surface of society, and in his *soma* rebellion he tries bravely to champion the virtues of individuality and freedom. But John is also an extremely contradictory character. He lashes out violently at others, is as intolerant of difference as those around him, and hypocritically refuses to act upon his own natural desires. While we might praise the battle he fights, we cannot truly consider him a heroic example of individuality. In many ways he is just as 'conditioned', just as irrational, as those he criticises.

From his first appearance in London, John proves to be an unsettling force. His mere presence causes several of the strict procedures of the society to malfunction: vials of spermatozoa, symbols of the artificial production of life, are upset during the laughter caused by his use of the 'smutty' word 'father'. Many citizens grow 'wild to see this delicious creature', with John inspiring an intensity of emotion the civilisation has worked hard to eradicate – but an intensity which seems only natural to humanity. John also embodies the different forms of social unrest felt by the other central characters, and inspires them to seek change. Lenina is not 'very keen on promiscuity lately' and in the end, as she arrives by helicopter at the lighthouse, we can see that John has inspired her to seek one lover over others. Helmholtz Watson wants to write 'something more important' than hypnopaedic rhymes, and through his obsession with the works of Shakespeare John helps him see the great potentials of art. In many ways he answers their unrest by embodying the change they both crave.

John's most deliberately heroic act is the *soma* rebellion, in which he disrupts one of the pillars of social control. *Soma* is an 'impenetrable wall between the actual universe and [people's] minds', and in depriving the citizens of it he hopes to awaken them to the reality of their subjugation.

While John's throwing the pills out of the window upsets the Deltas, who riot against his revolt, Helmholtz can see the act for what it is: a cry for liberty and freedom, and so he fights alongside John. The rebellion is quickly quashed, but the event is significant enough for the perpetrators to be called to Mustapha Mond's office. Mond, like Helmholtz, recognises that John's rebellious gesture threatens to set an example of freedom that endangers the strict order of the society of London. By causing this symbolic disruption, it is clear that John is a threat to the oppressive mechanisms of control and a potential champion of all those liberties and freedoms that have long been repressed.

Typical of Huxley's novel, however, John's status as a potential hero and champion of individuality is complicated by his violence and irrational behaviour. He brutally lashes out at Lenina in his apartment and at the lighthouse for following the passion he has inspired in her. These outbursts are not just expressions of his confused moral torment, but acts of irrational, childish violence. While he encourages others to follow their natural urges, he reacts against Lenina for following hers. Despite his abhorrence at the unnatural elements of life in London, he also hypocritically refuses to let himself follow his own natural desires, trying to condition himself out of his love for Lenina by jumping into a heath of juniper bushes, embracing 'an armful of green spikes' instead of 'the smooth body of his desires'.

It is also possible to view John as being as much a product of conditioning as those whose subservience and conformity he rails against. His frequent recitation of passages from Shakespeare is intended to parallel the similar use of hypnopaedic slogans in London. Rhymes such as 'a gramme is better than a damn' are used by people in London whenever they are in any doubt about what to do in a given situation, and John uses the words of Shakespeare in much the same fashion. Whenever he is faced with conflict he turns to these words in order to help him understand what he should do. As he contemplates Lenina's advances he is thrown into indecision until he remembers the words of Shakespeare that eventually motivate his violence: '"Whore!" he [shouts]. "Impudent strumpet!"'. When Mustapha Mond questions his views he proffers his defence by quoting from *King Lear* as if the truth of the world were contained in the words of the play. As much as the citizens of London understand their world through slogans, thinking these express essential truths, so John understands his reality through the plays of Shakespeare.

It cannot be denied that John thinks he has the best interests of the society at heart when he chooses to revolt. In several instances he does indeed inspire change, and helps other characters to articulate the restlessness and unhappiness they have been feeling. If we look closer at his character, however, we can see that he is not terribly unlike those he criticises. While he champions freedom and natural desire, he won't let himself love Lenina as he truly wants; while he is appalled by the mechanisms of hypnopaedia and brainwashing, he is arguably just as conditioned by the works of Shakespeare. While he thinks he fights the good fight, in the end he doesn't heroically transcend the world that he tries to flee.

REFERENCES & READING

Text

Huxley, Aldous 2006 (1932), *Brave New World*, Harper Perennial Modern Classics, New York.

References

Baker, R. 1990, Brave New World: *History, Science, and Dystopia*, Twayne Publishers, Boston.

Huxley, A. 1963, *Point Counter Point*, Chatto & Windus, London.

—— 1965, *Brave New World Revisited*, Chatto & Windus, London.

Pollerd, J. 2010, 'State versus the Individual: Civil Disobedience in *Brave New World*', in Harold Bloom, ed, *Civil Disobedience*, Chelsea House Publishers, New York.

Woiak, J. 2010, 'Designing a Brave New World: Eugenics, Politics, and Fiction' in Harold Bloom, ed, *Aldous Huxley*, Chelsea House Publishers, New York.

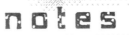
notes

CPSIA information can be obtained at www.ICGtesting.com
Printed in the USA
BVOW031213190212

283280BV00003B/5/P